OLD M

HOROSCOPE AND ASTRAL DIARY

PISCES

foulsham

LONDON • NEW YORK • TORONTO • SYDNEY

foulsham

The Publishing House, Bennetts Close,
Cippenham, Berks SL1 5AP

ISBN 0-572-03103-3

A CIP record for this book is available from the British Library

Printed in Great Britain by Cox & Wyman Ltd, Reading, Berkshire.

CONTENTS

INTRODUCTION

Astrology has been a part of life for centuries now, and no matter how technological our lives become, it seems that it never diminishes in popularity. For thousands of years people have been gazing up at the star-clad heavens and seeing their own activities and proclivities reflected in the movement of those little points of light. Across centuries countless hours have been spent studying the way our natures, activities and decisions seem to be paralleled by their predictable movements. Old Moore, a time-served veteran in astrological research, continues to monitor the zodiac and has produced the Astral Diary for 2006, tailor-made to your own astrological make-up.

Old Moore's Astral Diary is unique in its ability to get to the heart of your nature and to offer you the sort of advice that might come from a trusted friend. The Diaries are structured in such a way that you can see in a day-by-day sense exactly how the planets are working for you. The diary section advises how you can get the best from upcoming situations and allows you to plan ahead successfully. There is room in the daily sections to put your own observations or even appointments, and the book is conveniently structured to stay with you throughout the year.

Whilst other popular astrology books merely deal with your astrological 'Sun sign', the Astral Diaries go much further. Every person on the planet is unique, and Old Moore allows you to access your individuality in a number of ways. The front section gives you the chance to work out the placement of the Moon at the time of your birth and to see how its position has set an important seal on your overall nature. Perhaps most important of all, you can use the Astral Diary to discover your Rising Sign. This is the zodiac sign that was appearing over the Eastern horizon at the time of your birth and is just as important to you as an individual as is your Sun sign.

It is the synthesis of many different astrological possibilities that makes you what you are, and with the Astral Diaries you can learn so much. How do you react to love and romance? Through the unique Venus tables and the readings that follow them, you can learn where the planet Venus was at the time of your birth. It is even possible to register when little Mercury appears to be running retrograde, which can explain why you sometimes feel chatty, whilst at other moments you would rather withdraw into yourself. The Astral Diary will be an interest and a support throughout the whole year ahead.

Old Moore extends his customary greeting to all people of the Earth and offers his age-old wishes for a happy and prosperous period ahead.

THE ESSENCE
OF PISCES

Exploring the Personality of
Pisces the Fishes

(20TH FEBRUARY–20TH MARCH)

What's in a sign?

Pisceans are fascinating people – everyone you come across is likely to admit that fact. By nature you are kind, loving, trustful and inclined to work very hard on behalf of the people you love – and perhaps even those you don't like very much. Your nature is sympathetic and you will do anything you can to improve the lot of those you consider to be worse off than yourself. There is a very forgiving side to your temperament and also a strong artistic flair that can find an outlet in any one of a dozen different ways.

It's true you are difficult to know, and there is a very important reason for this. Your nature goes deep, so deep in fact that someone would have to live with you for a lifetime to plumb even a part of its fathomless depths. What the world sees is only ever a small part of the total magic of this most compulsive and fascinating zodiac sign. Much of your latent power and natural magic is constantly kept bottled up, because it is never your desire to manipulate those around you. Rather, you tend to wait in the shadows until opportunities to come into your own present themselves.

In love you are ardent and sincere, though sometimes inclined to choose a partner too readily and too early. There's a dreamy quality to your nature that makes you easy to adore, but which can also cause difficulties if the practical necessities of life take a very definite second place.

The chances are that you love music and picturesque scenery, and you may also exhibit a definite fondness for animals. You prefer to live in the country rather than in the middle of a noisy and smelly town, and tend to keep a reasonably well-ordered household. Your family can easily become your life and you always need a focus for your energies. You are not at all good at feathering your own nest, unless you know that someone else is also going to benefit on the way. A little more selfishness probably would not go amiss on occasions because you are often far too willing to put yourself out wholesale for people who don't respect your sacrifices. Pisceans can be full of raging passions and are some of the most misunderstood people to be found anywhere within the great circle of the zodiac.

Pisces resources

It is the very essence of your zodiac sign that you are probably sitting there and saying to yourself 'Resources? I have no resources'. Of course you are wrong, though it has to be admitted that a glaring self-confidence isn't likely to be listed amongst them. You are, however, a very deep thinker, and this can turn out to be a great advantage and a useful tool when it comes to getting on in life. Because your natural intuition is so strong (some people would call you psychic), you are rarely fooled by the glib words of others. Your own natural tendency to tell the truth can be a distinct advantage and a great help to you when it comes to getting on in life from a practical and financial viewpoint.

Whilst many of the signs of the zodiac tend to respond to life in an impulsive way, you are more likely to weigh up the pros and cons of any given situation very carefully. This means that when you do take action you can achieve much more success – as well as saving a good deal of energy on the way. People tend to confide in you automatically, so you are definitely at an advantage when it comes to knowing what makes your family and friends tick. At work you can labour quietly and confidently, either on your own or in the company of others. Some people would assert that Pisceans are model employees because you really do not know how to give anything less than your best.

Never underestimate the power of your instincts. Under most circumstances you are aware of the possible outcome of any given situation and should react as your inner mind dictates. Following this course inevitably puts you ahead of the game and explains why so quiet a sign can promote so many winners in life. Not that you are particularly competitive. It's much more important for you to be part of a winning team than to be out there collecting the glory for yourself.

You are dependable, kind, loving and peerless in your defence of those you take to. All of these are incredible resources when used in the correct way. Perhaps most important of all is your ability to get others on your side. In this you cannot be matched.

Beneath the surface

Everyone instinctively knows that there is something very important going on beneath the surface of the Piscean mind, though working out exactly what it might be is a different kettle of fish altogether. The fact is that you are very secretive about yourself and tend to give very little away. There are occasions when this tendency can be a saving grace, but others where it is definitely a great disadvantage. What isn't hard to see is your natural sympathy and your desire to help those in trouble. There's no end gain here, it's simply the way you are. Your inspiration to do anything is rarely rooted in what your own prize is likely to be. In your soul you are poetical, deeply romantic and inextricably tied to the forces and cycles of the world that brought you to birth.

Despite your capacity for single-minded concentration in some matters, you are often subject to mental confusion. Rational considerations often take second place to intuitive foresight and even inspiration. Making leaps in logic isn't at all unusual for you and forms part of the way you judge the world and deal with it.

If you really want to get on in life, and to gain the most you can from your interactions with others, you need to be very truthful in your approach. Somehow or other that means finding out what is really going on in your mind and explaining it to those around you. This is never going to be an easy process, partly because of your naturally secretive ways. Actually some astrologers overplay the tendency of Pisces to keep its secrets. A great deal of the time you simply don't think you have anything to say that would interest others and you always lack confidence in your own judgements. This is a shame because you rarely proceed without thinking carefully and don't often make glaring mistakes.

Many Pisceans develop an ingrained tendency to believe themselves inadequate in some way. Once again this is something you should fight against. Knowing others better, and allowing them to get to know you, might cause you to feel less quirky or strange. Whether you realise it or not you have a natural magnetism that draws others towards you. Try to spend rather less time thinking – though without losing that Piscean ability to meditate which is central to your well-being. If you allow the fascinating world of the Piscean mind to be shared by the people you come to trust, you should become more understandable to people who really want to like you even more.

Making the best of yourself

It must be remembered that the zodiac sign of Pisces represents two Fishes, tethered by a cord but constantly trying to break away from each other. This says a great deal about the basic Piscean nature. The inward, contemplative side of your personality is often at odds with the more gregarious and chatty qualities you also possess. Learning about this duality of nature can go at least part of the way towards dealing with it.

Although you often exhibit a distinct lack of self-confidence in your dealings with the world at large, you are, at heart, quite adept, flexible and able to cope under almost any circumstance. All that is really required in order to have a positive influence on life and to be successful is for you to realise what you are capable of achieving. Alas this isn't quite as easy as it might appear, because the introspective depths of your nature make you think too much and cause you to avoid the very actions that would get you noticed more. This can be something of a dilemma for Pisces, though it is certainly not insurmountable.

Never be afraid to allow your sensitivity to show. It is one of your greatest assets and it is part of the reason why other people love you so much – far more, in fact, than you probably realise. Your natural warmth, grace and charm are certain to turn heads on those occasions when you can't avoid being watched. The creative qualities that you possess make it possible for you to manufacture harmonious surroundings, both for yourself and for your family, who are very important to you. At the same time you recognise the practical in life and don't mind getting your hands dirty, especially when it comes to helping someone else out of a mess.

One of the best ruses Pisceans can use in order to get over the innate shyness that often attends the sign is to put on an act. Pisceans are very good natural actors and can easily assume the role of another individual. So, in your dealings with the world at large, manufacture a more confident individual, though without leaving out all the wonderful things that make you what you are now. Play this part for all you are worth and you will then truly be making the best of yourself.

The impressions you give

There is absolutely no doubt that you are more popular, admired and even fancied than you could ever believe. Such is the natural modesty of your zodiac sign that you invariably fail to pick up on those little messages coming across from other people that say 'I think you are wonderful'. If we don't believe in ourselves it's difficult for us to accept that others think we are worth their consideration. Failing to realise your worth to the world at large is likely to be your greatest fault and needs to be corrected.

In a way it doesn't matter, when seen from the perspective of others. What they observe is a warm-hearted individual. Your magnetic personality is always on display, whether you intend it to be or not, which is another reason why you tend to attract far more attention than you would sometimes elicit. Most Pisceans are quite sexy, another quality that is bound to come across to the people you meet, at least some of whom would be willing to jump through hoops if you were to command it.

In short, what you show, and what you think you are, could be two entirely different things. If you don't believe this to be the case you need to carry out a straw poll amongst some of the people you know. Ask them to write down all your qualities as they see them. The result will almost certainly surprise you and demonstrate that you are far more capable, and loveable, than you believe yourself to be. Armed with this knowledge you can walk forward in life with more confidence and feel as content inside as you appear to be when viewed by the world at large.

People rely heavily on you. That much at least you will have noticed in a day-to-day sense. They do so because they know how well you deal with almost any situation. Even in a crisis you show your true colours and that's part of the reason why so many Piscean people find themselves involved in the medical profession. You are viewed as being stronger than you believe yourself to be, which is why everyone tends to be so surprised when they discover that you are vulnerable and inclined to worry.

The way forward

You have a great deal to offer the world, even if you don't always appreciate how much. Although you are capable of being shy and introverted on occasions, you are equally likely to be friendly, chatty and very co-operative. You settle to just about any task, though you do possess a sense of freedom that makes it difficult for you to be cooped up in the same place for days and weeks at a stretch. You prefer the sort of tasks that allow your own natural proclivities to shine out, and you exhibit an instinctive creative tendency in almost anything you do.

Use your natural popularity to the full. People are always willing to put themselves out on your behalf, mainly because they know how generous you are and want to repay you for some previous favour. You should never be too proud to accept this sort of proffered help and must avoid running away with the idea that you are unequal to any reasonable task that you set yourself.

It's true that some of your thoughts are extremely deep and that you can get yourself into something of a brown study on occasions, which can be translated by the world around you as depression. However, you are far more stable than you probably believe yourself to be because Pisces is actually one of the toughest of the zodiac signs.

Because you are born of a Water sign it is likely that you would take great delight in living near the sea, or some other large body of water. This isn't essential to your well-being but it does feed your imagination. The vastness of nature in all its forms probably appeals to you in any case and most Pisceans love the natural world with its staggering diversity.

In love you are ardent and sincere, but you do need to make sure that you choose the right individual to suit you. Pisceans often settle for a protecting arm, but if this turns out to be stifling, trouble could follow. You would find it hard to live with anyone who didn't have at least a degree of your sensitivity, and you need a partner who will allow you to retain that sense of inner freedom that is so vital to your well-being.

Make the most of the many gifts and virtues that nature has bestowed upon you and don't be afraid to let people know what you really are. Actually establishing this in the first place isn't easy for you. Pisceans respond well to almost any form of meditation, which is not surprising because the sign of the Fishes is the most spiritually motivated zodiac sign of them all. When you know yourself fully you generate a personality that is an inspiration to everyone.

PISCES ON THE CUSP

Old Moore is often asked how astrological profiles are altered for those people born at either the beginning or the end of a zodiac sign, or, more properly, on the cusps of a sign. In the case of Pisces this would be on the 20th of February and for two or three days after, and similarly at the end of the sign, probably from the 18th to the 20th of March. In this year's Astral Diaries, once again, Old Moore sets out to explain the differences regarding cuspid signs.

The Aquarius Cusp – February 20th to 22nd

This tends to be a generally happy combination of signs, even if some of the people you come into contact with find you rather difficult to understand from time to time. You are quite capable of cutting a dash, as any Aquarian would be, and yet at the same time you have the quiet and contemplative qualities more typified by Pisces. You tend to be seen as an immensely attractive person, even if you are the last one in the world to accept this fact. People find you to be friendly, very approachable and good company in almost any social or personal setting. It isn't hard for you to get on with others, though since you are not so naturally quiet as Pisces when taken alone, you are slightly more willing to speak your mind and to help out, though usually in a very diplomatic manner.

At work you are very capable and many people with this combination find themselves working on behalf of humanity as a whole. Thus work in social services, hospitals or charities really suits the unique combinations thrown up by this sign mixture. Management is right up your street, though there are times when your conception of popularity takes the foremost place in your mind. Occasionally this could take the edge off executive decisions. A careful attention to detail shows you in a position to get things done, even jobs that others shun. You don't really care for getting your hands dirty but will tackle almost any task if you know it to be necessary. Being basically self-sufficient, you also love the company of others, and it is this adaptability that is the hallmark of success to Aquarian-cusp Pisceans.

Few people actually know you as well as they think they do because the waters of your nature run quite deep. Your real task in life is to let the world know how you feel, something you fight shy of doing now and again. There are positive gains in your life, brought about as a result of your adaptable and pleasing nature. Aquarius present in the nature allows Pisces to act at its best.

The Aries Cusp – March 18th to 20th

This is a Piscean with attitude and probably one of the most difficult zodiac sign combinations to be understood, not only by those people with whom you come into contact but clearly by yourself too. If there are any problems thrown up here they come from the fact that Pisces and Aries have such different ways of expressing themselves to the world at large. Aries is very upfront, dynamic and dominant, all factors that are simply diametrically opposed to the way Pisces thinks and behaves. So the real task in life is to find ways to combine the qualities of Pisces and Aries, in a way that suits the needs of both and without becoming totally confused with regard to your basic nature.

The problem is usually solved by a compartmentation of life. For example, many people with this combination will show the Aries qualities strongly at work, whilst dropping into the Piscean mode socially and at home. This may invariably be the case but there are bound to be times when the underlying motivations become mixed, which can confuse those with whom you come into contact.

Having said all of this you can be the least selfish and most successful individual when you are fighting for the rights of others. This is the zodiac combination of the true social reformer, the genuine politician and the committed pacifist. It seems paradoxical to suggest that someone could fight tenaciously for peace, but this is certainly true in your case. You have excellent executive skills and yet retain an ability to tell other people what they should be doing, in fairly strident terms, usually without upsetting anyone. There is a degree of genuine magic about you that makes you very attractive and there is likely to be more than one love affair in your life. A steadfast view of romance may not be naturally present within your basic nature but like so much else you can 'train' this quality into existence.

Personal success is likely, but it probably doesn't matter all that much in a material sense. The important thing to you is being needed by the world at large.

PISCES AND ITS ASCENDANTS

The nature of every individual on the planet is composed of the rich variety of zodiac signs and planetary positions that were present at the time of their birth. Your Sun sign, which in your case is Pisces, is one of the many factors when it comes to assessing the unique person you are. Probably the most important consideration, other than your Sun sign, is to establish the zodiac sign that was rising over the eastern horizon at the time that you were born. This is your Ascending or Rising sign. Most popular astrology fails to take account of the Ascendant, and yet its importance remains with you from the very moment of your birth, through every day of your life. The Ascendant is evident in the way you approach the world, and so, when meeting a person for the first time, it is this astrological influence that you are most likely to notice first. Our Ascending sign essentially represents what we appear to be, while the Sun sign is what we feel inside ourselves.

The Ascendant also has the potential for modifying our overall nature. For example, if you were born at a time of day when Pisces was passing over the eastern horizon (this would be around the time of dawn) then you would be classed as a double Pisces. As such, you would typify this zodiac sign, both internally and in your dealings with others. However, if your Ascendant sign turned out to be a Fire sign, such as Aries, there would be a profound alteration of nature, away from the expected qualities of Pisces.

One of the reasons why popular astrology often ignores the Ascendant is that it has always been rather difficult to establish. Old Moore has found a way to make this possible by devising an easy-to-use table, which you will find on page 157 of this book. Using this, you can establish your Ascendant sign at a glance. You will need to know your rough time of birth, then it is simply a case of following the instructions.

For those readers who have no idea of their time of birth it might be worth allowing a good friend, or perhaps your partner, to read through the section that follows this introduction. Someone who deals with you on a regular basis may easily discover your Ascending sign, even though you could have some difficulty establishing it for yourself. A good understanding of this component of your nature is essential if you want to be aware of that 'other person' who is responsible for the way you make contact with the world at large. Your Sun sign, Ascendant sign, and the other pointers in this book will, together, allow you a far better understanding of what makes you tick as an individual. Peeling back the different layers of your astrological make-up can be an enlightening experience, and the Ascendant may represent one of the most important layers of all.

Pisces with Pisces Ascendant

You are a kind and considerate person who would do almost anything to please the people around you. Creative and extremely perceptive, nobody knows the twists and turns of human nature better than you do, and you make it your business to serve humanity in any way you can. Not everyone understands what makes you tick, and part of the reason for this state of affairs is that you are often not really quite 'in' the world as much as the people you encounter in a day-to-day sense. At work you are generally cheerful, though you can be very quiet on occasions, but since you are consistent in this regard, you don't attract adverse attention or accusations of being moody, as some other variants of Pisces sometimes do. Confusion can beset you on occasions, especially when you are trying to reconcile your own opposing needs. There are certain moments of discontent to be encountered which so often come from trying to please others, even when to do so goes against your own instincts.

As age and experience add to your personal armoury you relax more with the world and find yourself constantly sought out for words of wisdom. The vast majority of people care for you deeply.

Pisces with Aries Ascendant

Although not an easy combination to deal with, the Pisces with an Aries Ascendant does bring something very special to the world in the way of natural understanding allied to practical assistance. It's true that you can sometimes be a dreamer, but there is nothing wrong with that as long as you have the ability to turn some of your wishes into reality, and this you are usually able to do, often for the sake of those around you. Conversation comes easily to you, though you also possess a slightly wistful and poetic side to your nature, which is attractive to the many people who call you a friend. A natural entertainer, you bring a sense of the comic to the often serious qualities of Aries, though without losing the determination that typifies the sign.

In relationships you are ardent, sincere and supportive, with a social conscience that sometimes finds you fighting the battles of the less privileged members of society. Family is important to you and this is a combination that invariably leads to parenthood. Away from the cut and thrust of everyday life you relax more fully, and think about matters more deeply than more typical Aries types might.

Pisces with Taurus Ascendant

You are clearly a very sensitive type of person and that sometimes makes it rather difficult for others to know how they might best approach you. Private and deep, you are nevertheless socially inclined on many occasions. However, because your nature is bottomless it is possible that some types would actually accuse you of being shallow. How can this come about? Well, it's simple really. The fact is that you rarely show anyone what is going on in the deepest recesses of your mind and so your responses can appear to be trite or even ill-considered. This is far from the truth, as those who are allowed into the 'inner sanctum' would readily admit. You are something of a sensualist, and relish staying in bed late and simply pleasing yourself for days on end. However, you have Taurean traits so you desire a tidy environment in which to live your usually long life.

You are able to deal with the routine aspects of life quite well and can be a capable worker once you are up and firing on all cylinders. It is very important that you maintain an interest in what you are doing, because the recesses of your dreamy mind can sometimes appear to be infinitely more attractive. Your imagination is second to none and this fact can often be turned to your advantage.

Pisces with Gemini Ascendant

There is great duality inherent in this combination, and sometimes this can cause a few problems. Part of the trouble stems from the fact that you often fail to realise what you want from life, and you could also be accused of failing to take the time out to think things through carefully enough. You are reactive, and although you have every bit of the natural charm that typifies the sign of Gemini, you are more prone to periods of self-doubt and confusion. However, you should not allow these facts to get you down too much, because you are also genuinely loved and have a tremendous capacity to look after others, a factor which is more important to you than any other. It's true that personal relationships can sometimes be a cause of difficulty for you, partly because your constant need to know what makes other people tick could drive them up the wall. Accepting people at face value seems to be the best key to happiness of a personal sort, and there are occasions when your very real and natural intuition has to be put on hold.

It's likely that you are an original, particularly in the way you dress. An early rebellious stage often gives way to a more comfortable form of eccentricity. When you are at your best, just about everyone adores you.

PISCES AND ITS ASCENDANTS

Pisces with Cancer Ascendant

A deep, double Water-sign combination this, and it might serve to make you a very misunderstood, though undoubtedly popular, individual. You are anxious to make a good impression, probably too keen under certain circumstances, and you do everything you can to help others, even if you don't know them very well. It's true that you are deeply sensitive and quite easily brought to tears by the suffering of this most imperfect world that we inhabit. Fatigue can be a problem, though this is somewhat nullified by the fact that you can withdraw completely into the deep recesses of your own mind when it becomes necessary to do so.

You may not be the most gregarious person in the world, simply because it isn't easy for you to put some of your most important considerations into words. This is easier when you are in the company of people you know and trust, though even trust is a commodity that is difficult for you to find, particularly since you may have been hurt by being too willing to share your thoughts early in life. With age comes wisdom and maturity, and the older you are, the better you will learn to handle this potent and demanding combination. You will never go short of either friends or would-be lovers, and may be one of the most magnetic types of both Cancer and Pisces.

Pisces with Leo Ascendant

You are a very sensitive soul, on occasions too much so for your own good. However, there is not a better advocate for the rights of humanity than you represent and you constantly do what you can to support the downtrodden and oppressed. Good causes are your thing and there are likely to be many in your life. You will probably find yourself pushed to the front of almost any enterprise of which you are a part because, despite the deeper qualities of Pisces, you are a natural leader. Even on those occasions when it feels as though you lack confidence, you manage to muddle through somehow and your smile is as broad as the day. Few sign combinations are more loved than this one, mainly because you do not have a malicious bone in your body, and will readily forgive and forget, which the Lion on its own often will not.

Although you are capable of acting on impulse, you do so from a deep sense of moral conviction, so that most of your endeavours are designed to suit other people too. They recognise this fact and will push much support back in your direction. Even when you come across troubles in your life you manage to find ways to sort them out, and will invariably notice something new to smile about on the way. Your sensitivity rating is massive and you can easily be moved to tears.

Pisces with Virgo Ascendant

You might have been accused on occasions of being too sensitive for your own good, a charge that is not entirely without foundation. Certainly you are very understanding of the needs of others, sometimes to the extent that you put everything aside to help them. This would also be true in the case of charities, for you care very much about the world and the people who cling tenaciously to its surface. Your ability to love on a one-to-one basis knows no bounds, though you may not discriminate as much as you could, particularly when young, and might have one or two false starts in the love stakes. You don't always choose to verbalise your thoughts and this can cause problems, because there is always so much going on in your mind and Virgo especially needs good powers of communication. Pisces is quieter and you need to force yourself to say what you think when the explanation is important.

You would never betray a confidence and sometimes take on rather more for the sake of your friends than is strictly good for you. This is not a fault but can cause you problems all the same. Because you are so intuitive there is little that escapes your attention, though you should avoid being pessimistic about your insights. Changes of scenery suit you and travel would bring out the best in what can be a repressed nature.

Pisces with Libra Ascendant

An Air and Water combination, you are not easy to understand and have depths that show at times, surprising those people who thought they already knew what you were. You will always keep people guessing and are just as likely to hitchhike around Europe as you are to hold down a steady job, both of which you would undertake with the same degree of commitment and success. Usually young at heart, but always carrying the potential for an old head on young shoulders, you are something of a paradox and not at all easy for totally 'straight' types to understand. But you always make an impression, and tend to be very attractive to members of the opposite sex.

In matters of health you do have to be a little careful because you dissipate much nervous energy and can sometimes be inclined to push yourself too hard, at least in a mental sense. Frequent periods of rest and meditation will do you the world of good and should improve your level of wisdom, which tends to be fairly high already. Much of your effort in life is expounded on behalf of humanity as a whole, for you care deeply, love totally and always give of your best. Whatever your faults and failings might be, you are one of the most popular people around.

Pisces with Scorpio Ascendant

You stand a chance of disappearing so deep into yourself that other people would need one of those long ladders that cave explorers use to even find you. It isn't really your fault, because both Scorpio and Pisces, as Water signs, are difficult to understand and you have them both. But that doesn't mean that you should be content to remain in the dark, and the warmth of your nature is all you need to shine a light on the wonderful qualities you possess. But the primary word of warning is that you must put yourself on display and allow others to know what you are, before their appreciation of these facts becomes apparent.

As a server of the world you are second to none and it is hard to find a person with this combination who is not, in some way, looking out for the people around them. Immensely attractive to others, you are also one of the most sought-after lovers. Much of this has to do with your deep and abiding charm, but the air of mystery that surrounds you also helps. Some of you will marry too early, and end up regretting the fact, though the majority of people with Scorpio and Pisces will find the love they deserve in the end. You are able, just, firm but fair, though a sucker for a hard luck story and as kind as the day is long. It's hard to imagine how so many good points could be ignored by others.

Pisces with Sagittarius Ascendant

A very attractive combination this, because the more dominant qualities of the Archer are somehow mellowed-out by the caring Water-sign qualities of the Fishes. You can be very outgoing, but there is always a deeper side to your nature that allows others to know that you are thinking about them. Few people could fall out with either your basic nature or your attitude to the world at large, even though there are depths to your nature that may not be easily understood. You are capable, have a good executive ability and can work hard to achieve your objectives, even if you get a little disillusioned on the way. Much of your life is given over to helping those around you and there is a great tendency for you to work for and on behalf of humanity as a whole. A sense of community is brought to most of what you do and you enjoy co-operation. Although you have the natural ability to attract people to you, the Pisces half of your nature makes you just a little more reserved in personal matters than might otherwise be the case. More careful in your choices than either sign taken alone, you still have to make certain that your motivations when commencing a personal relationship are the right ones. You love to be happy, and to offer gifts of happiness to others.

Pisces with Capricorn Ascendant

You are certainly not the easiest person in the world to understand, mainly because your nature is so deep and your personality so complicated, that others are somewhat intimidated at the prospect of staring into this abyss. All the same your friendly nature is attractive, and there will always be people around who are fascinated by the sheer magnetic quality that is intrinsic to this zodiac mix. Sentimental and extremely kind, there is no limit to the extent of your efforts on behalf of a deserving world, though there are some people around who wonder at your commitment and who may ridicule you a little for your staying-power, even in the face of some adversity. At work you are very capable, will work long and hard, and can definitely expect a greater degree of financial and practical success than Pisces when taken alone. Routines don't bother you too much, though you do need regular periods of introspection, which help to recharge low batteries and a battered self-esteem. In affairs of the heart you are given to impulse, which belies the more careful qualities of Capricorn. However, the determination remains intact and you are quite capable of chasing rainbows round and round the same field, never realising that you can't get to the end of them. Generally speaking you are an immensely lovable person and a great favourite to many.

Pisces with Aquarius Ascendant

Here we find the originality of Aquarius balanced by the very sensitive qualities of Pisces, and it makes for a very interesting combination. When it comes to understanding other people you are second to none, but it's certain that you are more instinctive than either Pisces or Aquarius when taken alone. You are better at routines than Aquarius, but also relish a challenge more than the typical Piscean would. Active and enterprising, you tend to know what you want from life, but consideration of others, and the world at large, will always be part of the scenario. People with this combination often work on behalf of humanity and are to be found in social work, the medical profession and religious institutions. As far as beliefs are concerned you don't conform to established patterns, and yet may get closer to the truth of the Creator than many deep theological thinkers have ever been able to do. Acting on impulse as much as you do means that not everyone understands the way your mind works, but your popularity will invariably see you through.

Passionate and deeply sensitive, you are able to negotiate the twists and turns of a romantic life that is hardly likely to be run-of-the-mill. In the end, however, you should certainly be able to find a very deep personal and spiritual happiness.

THE MOON AND THE PART IT PLAYS IN YOUR LIFE

In astrology the Moon is probably the single most important heavenly body after the Sun. Its unique position, as partner to the Earth on its journey around the solar system, means that the Moon appears to pass through the signs of the zodiac extremely quickly. The zodiac position of the Moon at the time of your birth plays a great part in personal character and is especially significant in the build-up of your emotional nature.

Sun Moon Cycles

The first lunar cycle deals with the part the position of the Moon plays relative to your Sun sign. I have made the fluctuations of this pattern easy for you to understand by means of a simple cyclic graph. It appears on the first page of each 'Your Month At A Glance', under the title 'Highs and Lows'. The graph displays the lunar cycle and you will soon learn to understand how its movements have a bearing on your level of energy and your abilities.

Your Own Moon Sign

Discovering the position of the Moon at the time of your birth has always been notoriously difficult because tracking the complex zodiac positions of the Moon is not easy. This process has been reduced to three simple stages with Old Moore's unique Lunar Tables. A breakdown of the Moon's zodiac positions can be found from page 23 onwards, so that once you know what your Moon Sign is, you can see what part this plays in the overall build-up of your personal character.

If you follow the instructions on the next page you will soon be able to work out exactly what zodiac sign the Moon occupied on the day that you were born and you can then go on to compare the reading for this position with those of your Sun sign and your Ascendant. It is partly the comparison between these three important positions that goes towards making you the unique individual you are.

HOW TO DISCOVER YOUR MOON SIGN

This is a three-stage process. You may need a pen and a piece of paper but if you follow the instructions below the process should only take a minute or so.

STAGE 1 First of all you need to know the Moon Age at the time of your birth. If you look at Moon Table 1, on page 21, you will find all the years between 1908 and 2006 down the left side. Find the year of your birth and then trace across to the right to the month of your birth. Where the two intersect you will find a number. This is the date of the New Moon in the month that you were born. You now need to count forward the number of days between the New Moon and your own birthday. For example, if the New Moon in the month of your birth was shown as being the 6th and you were born on the 20th, your Moon Age Day would be 14. If the New Moon in the month of your birth came after your birthday, you need to count forward from the New Moon in the previous month. If you were born in a Leap Year, remember to count the 29th February. You can tell if your birth year was a Leap Year if the last two digits can be divided by four. Whatever the result, jot this number down so that you do not forget it.

STAGE 2 Take a look at Moon Table 2 on page 22. Down the left hand column look for the date of your birth. Now trace across to the month of your birth. Where the two meet you will find a letter. Copy this letter down alongside your Moon Age Day.

STAGE 3 Moon Table 3 on page 22 will supply you with the zodiac sign the Moon occupied on the day of your birth. Look for your Moon Age Day down the left hand column and then for the letter you found in Stage 2. Where the two converge you will find a zodiac sign and this is the sign occupied by the Moon on the day that you were born.

Your Zodiac Moon Sign Explained

You will find a profile of all zodiac Moon Signs on pages 23 to 26, showing in yet another way how astrology helps to make you into the individual that you are. In each daily entry of the Astral Diary you can find the zodiac position of the Moon for every day of the year. This also allows you to discover your lunar birthdays. Since the Moon passes through all the signs of the zodiac in about a month, you can expect something like twelve lunar birthdays each year. At these times you are likely to be emotionally steady and able to make the sort of decisions that have real, lasting value.

MOON TABLE 1

YEAR	JAN	FEB	MAR	YEAR	JAN	FEB	MAR	YEAR	JAN	FEB	MAR
1908	3	2	3	1941	27	26	27	1974	24	22	24
1909	22	20	21	1942	16	15	16	1975	12	11	12
1910	11	9	11	1943	6	4	6	1976	1/31	29	30
1911	29	28	30	1944	25	24	24	1977	19	18	19
1912	18	17	19	1945	14	12	14	1978	9	7	9
1913	7	6	7	1946	3	2	3	1979	27	26	27
1914	25	24	26	1947	21	19	21	1980	16	15	16
1915	15	15	14	1948	11	9	11	1981	6	4	6
1916	5	3	5	1949	29	27	29	1982	25	23	24
1917	24	22	23	1950	18	16	18	1983	14	13	14
1918	12	11	12	1951	7	6	7	1984	3	1	2
1919	1/31	–	2/31	1952	26	25	25	1985	21	19	21
1920	21	19	20	1953	15	14	15	1986	10	9	10
1921	9	8	9	1954	5	3	5	1987	29	28	29
1922	27	26	28	1955	24	22	24	1988	18	17	18
1923	17	15	17	1956	13	11	12	1989	7	6	7
1924	6	5	5	1957	1/30	–	1/31	1990	26	25	26
1925	24	23	24	1958	19	18	20	1991	15	14	15
1926	14	12	14	1959	9	7	9	1992	4	3	4
1927	3	2	3	1960	27	26	27	1993	24	22	24
1928	21	19	21	1961	16	15	16	1994	11	10	12
1929	11	9	11	1962	6	5	6	1995	1/31	29	30
1930	29	28	30	1963	25	23	25	1996	19	18	19
1931	18	17	19	1964	14	13	14	1997	9	7	9
1932	7	6	7	1965	3	1	2	1998	27	26	27
1933	25	24	26	1966	21	19	21	1999	16	15	16
1934	15	14	15	1967	10	9	10	2000	6	4	6
1935	5	3	5	1968	29	28	29	2001	24	23	25
1936	24	22	23	1969	19	17	18	2002	13	12	13
1937	12	11	12	1970	7	6	7	2003	3	1	2
1938	1/31	–	2/31	1971	26	25	26	2004	21	20	21
1939	20	19	20	1972	15	14	15	2005	10	9	10
1940	9	8	9	1973	5	4	5	2006	29	28	29

TABLE 2

DAY	FEB	MAR
1	D	F
2	D	G
3	D	G
4	D	G
5	D	G
6	D	G
7	D	G
8	D	G
9	D	G
10	E	G
11	E	G
12	E	H
13	E	H
14	E	H
15	E	H
16	E	H
17	E	H
18	E	H
19	E	H
20	F	H
21	F	H
22	F	I
23	F	I
24	F	I
25	F	I
26	F	I
27	F	I
28	F	I
29	F	I
30	–	I
31	–	I

MOON TABLE 3

M/D	D	E	F	G	H	I	J
0	AQ	PI	PI	PI	AR	AR	AR
1	PI	PI	PI	AR	AR	AR	TA
2	PI	PI	AR	AR	AR	TA	TA
3	PI	AR	AR	AR	TA	TA	TA
4	AR	AR	AR	TA	TA	GE	GE
5	AR	TA	TA	TA	GE	GE	GE
6	TA	TA	TA	GE	GE	GE	CA
7	TA	TA	GE	GE	GE	CA	CA
8	TA	GE	GE	GE	CA	CA	CA
9	GE	GE	CA	CA	CA	CA	LE
10	GE	CA	CA	CA	LE	LE	LE
11	CA	CA	CA	LE	LE	LE	VI
12	CA	CA	LE	LE	LE	VI	VI
13	LE	LE	LE	LE	VI	VI	VI
14	LE	LE	VI	VI	VI	LI	LI
15	LE	VI	VI	VI	LI	LI	LI
16	VI	VI	VI	LI	LI	LI	SC
17	VI	VI	LI	LI	LI	SC	SC
18	VI	LI	LI	LI	SC	SC	SC
19	LI	LI	LI	SC	SC	SC	SA
20	LI	SC	SC	SC	SA	SA	SA
21	SC	SC	SC	SA	SA	SA	CP
22	SC	SC	SA	SA	SA	CP	CP
23	SC	SA	SA	SA	CP	CP	CP
24	SA	SA	SA	CP	CP	CP	AQ
25	SA	CP	CP	CP	AQ	AQ	AQ
26	CP	CP	CP	AQ	AQ	AQ	PI
27	CP	AQ	AQ	AQ	AQ	PI	PI
28	AQ	AQ	AQ	AQ	PI	PI	PI
29	AQ	AQ	AQ	PI	PI	PI	AR

AR = Aries, TA = Taurus, GE = Gemini, CA = Cancer, LE = Leo, VI = Virgo, LI = Libra, SC = Scorpio, SA = Sagittarius, CP = Capricorn, AQ = Aquarius, PI = Pisces

MOON SIGNS

Moon in Aries

You have a strong imagination, courage, determination and a desire to do things in your own way and forge your own path through life.

Originality is a key attribute; you are seldom stuck for ideas although your mind is changeable and you could take the time to focus on individual tasks. Often quick-tempered, you take orders from few people and live life at a fast pace. Avoid health problems by taking regular time out for rest and relaxation.

Emotionally, it is important that you talk to those you are closest to and work out your true feelings. Once you discover that people are there to help, there is less necessity for you to do everything yourself.

Moon in Taurus

The Moon in Taurus gives you a courteous and friendly manner, which means you are likely to have many friends.

The good things in life mean a lot to you, as Taurus is an Earth sign that delights in experiences which please the senses. Hence you are probably a lover of good food and drink, which may in turn mean you need to keep an eye on the bathroom scales, especially as looking good is also important to you.

Emotionally you are fairly stable and you stick by your own standards. Taureans do not respond well to change. Intuition also plays an important part in your life.

Moon in Gemini

You have a warm-hearted character, sympathetic and eager to help others. At times reserved, you can also be articulate and chatty: this is part of the paradox of Gemini, which always brings duplicity to the nature. You are interested in current affairs, have a good intellect, and are good company and likely to have many friends. Most of your friends have a high opinion of you and would be ready to defend you should the need arise. However, this is usually unnecessary, as you are quite capable of defending yourself in any verbal confrontation.

Travel is important to your inquisitive mind and you find intellectual stimulus in mixing with people from different cultures. You also gain much from reading, writing and the arts but you do need plenty of rest and relaxation in order to avoid fatigue.

Moon in Cancer

The Moon in Cancer at the time of birth is a fortunate position as Cancer is the Moon's natural home. This means that the qualities of compassion and understanding given by the Moon are especially enhanced in your nature, and you are friendly and sociable and cope well with emotional pressures. You cherish home and family life, and happily do the domestic tasks. Your surroundings are important to you and you hate squalor and filth. You are likely to have a love of music and poetry.

Your basic character, although at times changeable like the Moon itself, depends on symmetry. You aim to make your surroundings comfortable and harmonious, for yourself and those close to you.

Moon in Leo

The best qualities of the Moon and Leo come together to make you warm-hearted, fair, ambitious and self-confident. With good organisational abilities, you invariably rise to a position of responsibility in your chosen career. This is fortunate as you don't enjoy being an 'also-ran' and would rather be an important part of a small organisation than a menial in a large one.

You should be lucky in love, and happy, provided you put in the effort to make a comfortable home for yourself and those close to you. It is likely that you will have a love of pleasure, sport, music and literature. Life brings you many rewards, most of them as a direct result of your own efforts, although you may be luckier than average and ready to make the best of any situation.

Moon in Virgo

You are endowed with good mental abilities and a keen receptive memory, but you are never ostentatious or pretentious. Naturally quite reserved, you still have many friends, especially of the opposite sex. Marital relationships must be discussed carefully and worked at so that they remain harmonious, as personal attachments can be a problem if you do not give them your full attention.

Talented and persevering, you possess artistic qualities and are a good homemaker. Earning your honours through genuine merit, you work long and hard towards your objectives but show little pride in your achievements. Many short journeys will be undertaken in your life.

Moon in Libra

With the Moon in Libra you are naturally popular and make friends easily. People like you, probably more than you realise, you bring fun to a party and are a natural diplomat. For all its good points, Libra is not the most stable of astrological signs and, as a result, your emotions can be a little unstable too. Therefore, although the Moon in Libra is said to be good for love and marriage, your Sun sign and Rising sign will have an important effect on your emotional and loving qualities.

You must remember to relate to others in your decision-making. Co-operation is crucial because Libra represents the 'balance' of life that can only be achieved through harmonious relationships. Conformity is not easy for you because Libra, an Air sign, likes its independence.

Moon in Scorpio

Some people might call you pushy. In fact, all you really want to do is to live life to the full and protect yourself and your family from the pressures of life. Take care to avoid giving the impression of being sarcastic or impulsive and use your energies wisely and constructively.

You have great courage and you invariably achieve your goals by force of personality and sheer effort. You are fond of mystery and are good at predicting the outcome of situations and events. Travel experiences can be beneficial to you.

You may experience problems if you do not take time to examine your motives in a relationship, and also if you allow jealousy, always a feature of Scorpio, to cloud your judgement.

Moon in Sagittarius

The Moon in Sagittarius helps to make you a generous individual with humanitarian qualities and a kind heart. Restlessness may be intrinsic as your mind is seldom still. Perhaps because of this, you have a need for change that could lead you to several major moves during your adult life. You are not afraid to stand your ground when you know your judgement is right, you speak directly and have good intuition.

At work you are quick, efficient and versatile and so you make an ideal employee. You need work to be intellectually demanding and do not enjoy tedious routines.

In relationships, you anger quickly if faced with stupidity or deception, though you are just as quick to forgive and forget. Emotionally, there are times when your heart rules your head.

Moon in Capricorn

The Moon in Capricorn makes you popular and likely to come into the public eye in some way. The watery Moon is not entirely comfortable in the Earth sign of Capricorn and this may lead to some difficulties in the early years of life. An initial lack of creative ability and indecision must be overcome before the true qualities of patience and perseverance inherent in Capricorn can show through.

You have good administrative ability and are a capable worker, and if you are careful you can accumulate wealth. But you must be cautious and take professional advice in partnerships, as you are open to deception. You may be interested in social or welfare work, which suit your organisational skills and sympathy for others.

Moon in Aquarius

The Moon in Aquarius makes you an active and agreeable person with a friendly, easy-going nature. Sympathetic to the needs of others, you flourish in a laid-back atmosphere. You are broad-minded, fair and open to suggestion, although sometimes you have an unconventional quality which others can find hard to understand.

You are interested in the strange and curious, and in old articles and places. You enjoy trips to these places and gain much from them. Political, scientific and educational work interests you and you might choose a career in science or technology.

Money-wise, you make gains through innovation and concentration and Lunar Aquarians often tackle more than one job at a time. In love you are kind and honest.

Moon in Pisces

You have a kind, sympathetic nature, somewhat retiring at times, but you always take account of others' feelings and help when you can.

Personal relationships may be problematic, but as life goes on you can learn from your experiences and develop a better understanding of yourself and the world around you.

You have a fondness for travel, appreciate beauty and harmony and hate disorder and strife. You may be fond of literature and would make a good writer or speaker yourself. You have a creative imagination and may come across as an incurable romantic. You have strong intuition, maybe bordering on a mediumistic quality, which sets you apart from the mass. You may not be rich in cash terms, but your personal gifts are worth more than gold.

PISCES IN LOVE

Discover how compatible in love you are with people from the same and other signs of the zodiac. Five stars equals a match made in heaven!

Pisces meets Pisces

Pisceans are easy-going and get on well with most people, so when two Pisceans get together, harmony is invariably the result. While this isn't the most dynamic relationship, there is mutual understanding, and a desire to please on both sides. Neither partner is likely to be overbearing or selfish. Family responsibilities should be happily shared and home surroundings will be comfortable, but never pretentious. One of the better pairings for the sign of the Fishes. Star rating: *****

Pisces meets Aries

Still waters run deep, and they don't come much deeper than Pisces. Although these signs share the same quadrant of the zodiac, they have little in common. Pisces is a dreamer, a romantic idealist with steady and spiritual goals. Aries needs to be on the move, and has very different ideals. It's hard to see how a relationship could develop but, with patience, there is a chance that things might work out. Pisces needs incentive, and Aries may be the sign to offer it. Star rating: **

Pisces meets Taurus

No problem here, unless both parties come from the quieter side of their respective signs. Most of the time Taurus and Pisces would live comfortably together, offering mutual support and deep regard. Taurus can offer the personal qualities that Pisces craves, whilst Pisces understands and copes with the Bull's slightly stubborn qualities. Taurus is likely to travel in Piscean company, so there is a potential for wide-ranging experiences and variety which is essential. There will be some misunderstandings, mainly because Pisces is so deep, but that won't prevent their enduring happiness. Star rating: ***

Pisces meets Gemini

Gemini likes to think of itself as intuitive and intellectual, but it will never understand Pisces' dark depths. Another stumbling block is that both Gemini and Pisces are 'split' signs – the Twins and the two Fishes – which means that both are capable of dual personalities. There won't be any shortage of affection, but the real question has to be how much these people feel they have in common. Pisces is extremely kind, and so is Gemini most of the time. But Pisces does too much soul-searching for Gemini, who might eventually become bored. Star rating: ***

Pisces meets Cancer

This is likely to be a very successful match. Cancer and Pisces are both Water signs, both deep, sensitive and very caring. Pisces loves deeply, and Cancer wants to be loved. There will be few fireworks here, and a very quiet house. But that doesn't mean that either love or action is lacking – the latter of which is just behind closed doors. Family and children are important to both signs and both are prepared to work hard, but Pisces is the more restless of the two and needs the support and security that Cancer offers. Star rating: *****

Pisces meets Leo

Pisces always needs to understand others, which makes Leo feel warm and loved, while Leo sees, to its delight, that Pisces needs to be protected and taken care of. Pisceans are often lacking in self-confidence which is something Leo has to spare, and happily it is often infectious. Pisces' inevitable cares are swept away on a tide of Leonine cheerfulness. This couple's home would be cheerful and full of love, which is beneficial to all family members. This is not a meeting of minds, but rather an understanding and appreciation of differences. Star rating: ****

Pisces meets Virgo

This looks an unpromising match from beginning to end. There are exceptions to every rule, particularly where Pisces is concerned, but these two signs are both so deep it's hard to imagine that they could ever find what makes the other tick. The depth is different in each case: Virgo's ruminations are extremely materialistic, while Pisces exists in a world of deep-felt, poorly expressed emotion. Pisces and Virgo might find they don't talk much, so only in a contemplative, almost monastic, match would they ever get on. Still, in a vast zodiac, anything is possible. Star rating: **

Pisces meets Libra

Libra and Pisces can be extremely fond of each other, even deeply in love, but this alone isn't a stable foundation for long-term success. Pisces is extremely deep and doesn't even know itself very well. Libra may initially find this intriguing but will eventually feel frustrated at being unable to understand the Piscean's emotional and personal feelings. Pisces can be jealous and may find Libra's flightiness difficult, which Libra can't stand. They are great friends and they may make it to the romantic stakes, but when they get there a great deal of effort will be necessary. Star rating: ***

Pisces meets Scorpio

If ever there were two zodiac signs that have a total rapport, it has to be Scorpio and Pisces. They share very similar needs: they are not gregarious and are happy with a little silence, good music and time to contemplate the finer things in life, and both are attracted to family life. Apart, they can have a tendency to wander in a romantic sense, but this is reduced when they come together. They are deep, firm friends who enjoy each other's company and this must lead to an excellent chance of success. These people are surely made for each other! Star rating: *****

Pisces meets Sagittarius

Probably the least likely success story for either sign, which is why it scores so low on the star rating. The basic problem is an almost total lack of understanding. A successful relationship needs empathy and progress towards a shared goal but, although both are eager to please, Pisces is too deep and Sagittarius too flighty – they just don't belong on the same planet! As pals, they have more in common and so a friendship is the best hope of success and happiness. Star rating: *

Pisces meets Capricorn

There is some chance of a happy relationship here, but it will need work on both sides. Capricorn is a go-getter, but likes to plan long term. Pisces is naturally more immediate, but has enough intuition to understand the Goat's thinking. Both have patience, but it will usually be Pisces who chooses to play second fiddle. The quiet nature of both signs might be a problem, as someone will have to take the lead, especially in social situations. Both signs should recognise this fact and accommodate it. Star rating: ***

Pisces meets Aquarius

Zodiac signs that follow each other often have something in common, but this is often not the case with Aquarius and Pisces. Both signs are deeply caring, but in different ways. Pisces is one of the deepest zodiac signs, and Aquarius simply isn't prepared to embark on the journey. Pisceans, meanwhile, would probably find Aquarians superficial and even flippant. On the positive side, there is potential for a well-balanced relationship, but unless one party is untypical of their zodiac sign, it often doesn't get started. Star rating: **

VENUS:
THE PLANET OF LOVE

If you look up at the sky around sunset or sunrise you will often see Venus in close attendance to the Sun. It is arguably one of the most beautiful sights of all and there is little wonder that historically it became associated with the goddess of love. But although Venus does play an important part in the way you view love and in the way others see you romantically, this is only one of the spheres of influence that it enjoys in your overall character.

Venus has a part to play in the more cultured side of your life and has much to do with your appreciation of art, literature, music and general creativity. Even the way you look is responsive to the part of the zodiac that Venus occupied at the start of your life, though this fact is also down to your Sun sign and Ascending sign. If, at the time you were born, Venus occupied one of the more gregarious zodiac signs, you will be more likely to wear your heart on your sleeve, as well as to be more attracted to entertainment, social gatherings and good company. If on the other hand Venus occupied a quiet zodiac sign at the time of your birth, you would tend to be more retiring and less willing to shine in public situations.

It's good to know what part the planet Venus plays in your life for it can have a great bearing on the way you appear to the rest of the world and since we all have to mix with others, you can learn to make the very best of what Venus has to offer you.

One of the great complications in the past has always been trying to establish exactly what zodiac position Venus enjoyed when you were born because the planet is notoriously difficult to track. However, I have solved that problem by creating a table that is exclusive to your Sun sign, which you will find on the following page.

Establishing your Venus sign could not be easier. Just look up the year of your birth on the page opposite and you will see a sign of the zodiac. This was the sign that Venus occupied in the period covered by your sign in that year. If Venus occupied more than one sign during the period, this is indicated by the date on which the sign changed, and the name of the new sign. For instance, if you were born in 1940, Venus was in Aries until the 9th March, after which time it was in Taurus. If you were born before 9th March your Venus sign is Aries, if you were born on or after 9th March, your Venus sign is Taurus. Once you have established the position of Venus at the time of your birth, you can then look in the pages which follow to see how this has a bearing on your life as a whole.

1908 ARIES / 11.3 TAURUS
1909 AQUARIUS / 5.3 PISCES
1910 AQUARIUS
1911 PISCES / 27.2 ARIES
I912 CAPRICORN /
   24.2 AQUARIUS / 19.3 PISCES
1913 ARIES / 7.3 TAURUS
1914 PISCES / 15.3 ARIES
1915 CAPRICORN
1916 ARIES / 10.3 TAURUS
1917 AQUARIUS / 5.3 PISCES
1918 AQUARIUS
1919 PISCES / 27.2 ARIES
1920 CAPRICORN /
   24.2 AQUARIUS / 19.3 PISCES
1921 ARIES / 8.3 TAURUS
1922 PISCES / 14.3 ARIES
1923 CAPRICORN
1924 ARIES / 10.3 TAURUS
1925 AQUARIUS / 4.3 PISCES
1926 AQUARIUS
1927 PISCES / 26.2 ARIES
1928 CAPRICORN /
   23.2 AQUARIUS / 18.3 PISCES
1929 ARIES / 9.3 TAURUS
1930 PISCES / 13.3 ARIES
1931 CAPRICORN
1932 ARIES / 9.3 TAURUS
1933 AQUARIUS / 4.3 PISCES
1934 AQUARIUS
1935 PISCES / 25.2 ARIES
1936 CAPRICORN /
   23.2 AQUARIUS / 18.3 PISCES
1937 ARIES / 10.3 TAURUS
1938 PISCES / 12.3 ARIES
1939 CAPRICORN
1940 ARIES / 9.3 TAURUS
1941 AQUARIUS / 3.3 PISCES
1942 AQUARIUS
1943 PISCES / 25.2 ARIES
1944 CAPRICORN /
   22.2 AQUARIUS / 18.3 PISCES
1945 ARIES / 11.3 TAURUS
1946 PISCES / 11.3 ARIES
1947 CAPRICORN
1948 ARIES / 8.3 TAURUS
1949 AQUARIUS / 3.3 PISCES
1950 AQUARIUS
1951 PISCES / 24.2 ARIES
1952 CAPRICORN /
   22.2 AQUARIUS / 17.3 PISCES
1953 ARIES
1954 PISCES / 11.3 ARIES
1955 CAPRICORN
1956 ARIES / 8.3 TAURUS
1957 AQUARIUS / 2.3 PISCES
1958 CAPRICORN /
   25.2 AQUARIUS
1959 PISCES / 24.2 ARIES

1960 CAPRICORN /
   21.2 AQUARIUS / 17.3 PISCES
1961 ARIES
1962 PISCES / 10.3 ARIES
1963 CAPRICORN
1964 ARIES / 8.3 TAURUS
1965 AQUARIUS / 1.3 PISCES
1966 AQUARIUS
1967 PISCES / 23.2 ARIES
1968 SAGITTARIUS /
   26.1 CAPRICORN
1969 ARIES
1970 PISCES / 10.3 ARIES
1971 CAPRICORN
1972 ARIES / 7.3 TAURUS
1973 AQUARIUS / 1.3 PISCES
1974 CAPRICORN / 2.3 AQUARIUS
1975 PISCES / 23.2 ARIES
1976 SAGITTARIUS /
   26.1 CAPRICORN
1977 ARIES
1978 PISCES / 9.3 ARIES
1979 CAPRICORN
1980 ARIES / 7.3 TAURUS
1981 AQUARIUS / 28.2 PISCES
1982 CAPRICORN / 4.3 AQUARIUS
1983 PISCES / 23.2 ARIES
1984 SAGITTARIUS /
   25.1 CAPRICORN
1985 ARIES
1986 PISCES / 9.3 ARIES
1987 CAPRICORN
1988 ARIES / 7.3 TAURUS
1989 AQUARIUS / 28.2 PISCES
1990 CAPRICORN / 5.3 AQUARIUS
1991 PISCES / 22.2 ARIES /
   20.3 TAURUS
1992 SAGITTARIUS /
   25.1 CAPRICORN
1993 ARIES
1994 PISCES / 9.3 ARIES
1995 CAPRICORN
1996 ARIES / 7.3 TAURUS
1997 AQUARIUS / 27.2 PISCES
1998 CAPRICORN / 5.3 AQUARIUS
1999 PISCES / 22.2 ARIES /
   19.3 TAURUS
2000 SAGITTARIUS /
   25.1 CAPRICORN
2001 ARIES
2002 PISCES / 9.3 ARIES
2003 CAPRICORN
2004 ARIES / 7.3 TAURUS
2005 AQUARIUS / 27.2 PISCES
2006 CAPRICORN / 5.3 AQUARIUS

VENUS THROUGH THE ZODIAC SIGNS

Venus in Aries

Amongst other things, the position of Venus in Aries indicates a fondness for travel, music and all creative pursuits. Your nature tends to be affectionate and you would try not to create confusion or difficulty for others if it could be avoided. Many people with this planetary position have a great love of the theatre, and mental stimulation is of the greatest importance. Early romantic attachments are common with Venus in Aries, so it is very important to establish a genuine sense of romantic continuity. Early marriage is not recommended, especially if it is based on sympathy. You may give your heart a little too readily on occasions.

Venus in Taurus

You are capable of very deep feelings and your emotions tend to last for a very long time. This makes you a trusting partner and lover, whose constancy is second to none. In life you are precise and careful and always try to do things the right way. Although this means an ordered life, which you are comfortable with, it can also lead you to be rather too fussy for your own good. Despite your pleasant nature, you are very fixed in your opinions and quite able to speak your mind. Others are attracted to you and historical astrologers always quoted this position of Venus as being very fortunate in terms of marriage. However, if you find yourself involved in a failed relationship, it could take you a long time to trust again.

Venus in Gemini

As with all associations related to Gemini, you tend to be quite versatile, anxious for change and intelligent in your dealings with the world at large. You may gain money from more than one source but you are equally good at spending it. There is an inference here that you are a good communicator, via either the written or the spoken word, and you love to be in the company of interesting people. Always on the look-out for culture, you may also be very fond of music, and love to indulge the curious and cultured side of your nature. In romance you tend to have more than one relationship and could find yourself associated with someone who has previously been a friend or even a distant relative.

Venus in Cancer

You often stay close to home because you are very fond of family and enjoy many of your most treasured moments when you are with those you love. Being naturally sympathetic, you will always do anything you can to support those around you, even people you hardly know at all. This charitable side of your nature is your most noticeable trait and is one of the reasons why others are naturally so fond of you. Being receptive and in some cases even psychic, you can see through to the soul of most of those with whom you come into contact. You may not commence too many romantic attachments but when you do give your heart, it tends to be unconditionally.

Venus in Leo

It must become quickly obvious to almost anyone you meet that you are kind, sympathetic and yet determined enough to stand up for anyone or anything that is truly important to you. Bright and sunny, you warm the world with your natural enthusiasm and would rarely do anything to hurt those around you, or at least not intentionally. In romance you are ardent and sincere, though some may find your style just a little overpowering. Gains come through your contacts with other people and this could be especially true with regard to romance, for love and money often come hand in hand for those who were born with Venus in Leo. People claim to understand you, though you are more complex than you seem.

Venus in Virgo

Your nature could well be fairly quiet no matter what your Sun sign might be, though this fact often manifests itself as an inner peace and would not prevent you from being basically sociable. Some delays and even the odd disappointment in love cannot be ruled out with this planetary position, though it's a fact that you will usually find the happiness you look for in the end. Catapulting yourself into romantic entanglements that you know to be rather ill-advised is not sensible, and it would be better to wait before you committed yourself exclusively to any one person. It is the essence of your nature to serve the world at large and through doing so it is possible that you will attract money at some stage in your life.

Venus in Libra

Venus is very comfortable in Libra and bestows upon those people who have this planetary position a particular sort of kindness that is easy to recognise. This is a very good position for all sorts of friendships and also for romantic attachments that usually bring much joy into your life. Few individuals with Venus in Libra would avoid marriage and since you are capable of great depths of love, it is likely that you will find a contented personal life. You like to mix with people of integrity and intelligence but don't take kindly to scruffy surroundings or work that means getting your hands too dirty. Careful speculation, good business dealings and money through marriage all seem fairly likely.

Venus in Scorpio

You are quite open and tend to spend money quite freely, even on those occasions when you don't have very much. Although your intentions are always good, there are times when you get yourself in to the odd scrape and this can be particularly true when it comes to romance, which you may come to late or from a rather unexpected direction. Certainly you have the power to be happy and to make others contented on the way, but you find the odd stumbling block on your journey through life and it could seem that you have to work harder than those around you. As a result of this, you gain a much deeper understanding of the true value of personal happiness than many people ever do, and are likely to achieve true contentment in the end.

Venus in Sagittarius

You are lighthearted, cheerful and always able to see the funny side of any situation. These facts enhance your popularity, which is especially high with members of the opposite sex. You should never have to look too far to find romantic interest in your life, though it is just possible that you might be too willing to commit yourself before you are certain that the person in question is right for you. Part of the problem here extends to other areas of life too. The fact is that you like variety in everything and so can tire of situations that fail to offer it. All the same, if you choose wisely and learn to understand your restless side, then great happiness can be yours.

Venus in Capricorn

The most notable trait that comes from Venus in this position is that it makes you trustworthy and able to take on all sorts of responsibilities in life. People are instinctively fond of you and love you all the more because you are always ready to help those who are in any form of need. Social and business popularity can be yours and there is a magnetic quality to your nature that is particularly attractive in a romantic sense. Anyone who wants a partner for a lover, a spouse and a good friend too would almost certainly look in your direction. Constancy is the hallmark of your nature and unfaithfulness would go right against the grain. You might sometimes be a little too trusting.

Venus in Aquarius

This location of Venus offers a fondness for travel and a desire to try out something new at every possible opportunity. You are extremely easy to get along with and tend to have many friends from varied backgrounds, classes and inclinations. You like to live a distinct sort of life and gain a great deal from moving about, both in a career sense and with regard to your home. It is not out of the question that you could form a romantic attachment to someone who comes from far away or be attracted to a person of a distinctly artistic and original nature. What you cannot stand is jealousy, for you have friends of both sexes and would want to keep things that way.

Venus in Pisces

The first thing people tend to notice about you is your wonderful, warm smile. Being very charitable by nature you will do anything to help others, even if you don't know them well. Much of your life may be spent sorting out situations for other people, but it is very important to feel that you are living for yourself too. In the main, you remain cheerful, and tend to be quite attractive to members of the opposite sex. Where romantic attachments are concerned, you could be drawn to people who are significantly older or younger than yourself or to someone with a unique career or point of view. It might be best for you to avoid marrying whilst you are still very young.

THE ASTRAL DIARY
HOW THE DIAGRAMS WORK

Through the picture diagrams in the Astral Diary I want to help you to plot your year. With them you can see where the positive and negative aspects will be found in each month. To make the most of them, all you have to do is remember where and when!

Let me show you how they work ...

THE MONTH AT A GLANCE

Just as there are twelve separate zodiac signs, so astrologers believe that each sign has twelve separate aspects to life. Each of the twelve segments relates to a different personal aspect. I list them all every month so that their meanings are always clear.

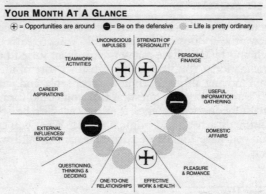

I have designed this chart to show you how and when these twelve different aspects are being influenced throughout the year. When there is a shaded circle, nothing out of the ordinary is to be expected. However, when a circle turns white with a plus sign, the influence is positive. Where the circle is black with a minus sign, it is a negative.

YOUR ENERGY RHYTHM CHART

On the opposite page is a picture diagram in which I am linking your zodiac group to the rhythm of the Moon. In doing this I have calculated when you will be gaining strength from its influence and equally when you may be weakened by it.

If you think of yourself as being like the tides of the ocean then you may understand how your own energies must also rise and fall. And if you understand how it works and when it is working, then you can better organise your activities to achieve more and get things done more easily.

YOUR ENERGY RHYTHM CHART

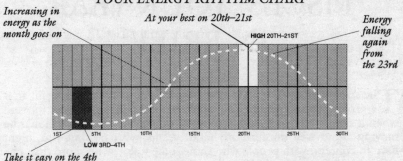

Increasing in energy as the month goes on

At your best on 20th–21st

HIGH 20TH–21ST

Energy falling again from the 23rd

LOW 3RD–4TH

Take it easy on the 4th

MOVING PICTURE SCREEN
Love, money, career and vitality measured every week

The diagram at the end of each week is designed to be informative and fun. The arrows move up and down the scale to give you an idea of the strength of your opportunities in each area. If LOVE stands at plus 4, then get out and put yourself about because things are going your way in romance! The further down the arrow goes, the weaker the opportunities. Do note that the diagram is an overall view of your astrological aspects and therefore reflects a trend which may not concur with every day in that cycle.

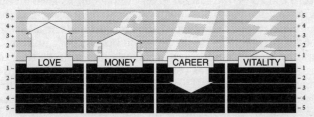

AND FINALLY:

am ....

pm ....

The two lines that are left blank in each daily entry of the Astral Diary are for your own personal use. You may find them ideal for keeping a check on birthdays or appointments, though it could be an idea to make notes from the astrological trends and diagrams a few weeks in advance. Some of the lines are marked with a key, which indicates the working of astrological cycles in your life. Look out for them each week as they are the best days to take action or make decisions. The daily text tells you which area of your life to focus on.

☿ = Mercury is retrograde on that day.

PISCES: YOUR YEAR IN BRIEF

The start of the year should find you anxious to get going again after a prolonged lay-off and you won't be backward at coming forward when it comes to making an impression on life. At work you should be moving ahead well during both January and February, but you might have to contend with people who show some jealousy on more than one occasion. Finances should be strong after you get over the shock of what Christmas did to your bank account!

With the arrival of the spring, March and April bring a generally happy frame of mind and a desire to push the bounds of the credible. You have more to say for yourself and the quieter side of Pisces is definitely taking a holiday. Love matches work out well, and for those with existing attachments, you have the chance to create a perfect environment for your lover. As throughout most of this year, intuition counts for a great deal.

Although you will begin May with a good deal of optimism, not everything will seem to be going your way as the month unfolds. There are quiet spells and times when you think your plans are failing but this won't turn out to be the case. It is very important to keep an open mind so that when June begins, you will be in the right place and the correct frame of mind to make the best of any eventuality. June also finds you in the mood for travel, so a hastily arranged holiday isn't unlikely.

With the high summer you won't have quite as much time to address the practical aspects of life as you might wish, but that is because you are enjoying yourself so much. There are new social possibilities throughout July and August, together with a continued desire for travel that is hard to ignore. August might bring some extra cash, probably as a result of surprising circumstances.

September is one of the happiest months of the year all round for Pisces. You will be raring to go, keen to make a good impression and luckier than might sometimes be the case. Although the month of October is quieter, it carries a good deal of confidence for you and sees you advancing on most fronts.

Don't give so much of yourself to others during November that you forget about your own needs. This is a trait that is strong for Pisceans and at this time you might have to be just a little selfish if you want to achieve your objectives. It will take you a little while during December to get into the Christmas spirit but when you do there is no holding you back. Nostalgia and excitement alternate as Christmas Day approaches, and the holidays should be memorable.

January 2006

YOUR MONTH AT A GLANCE

⊕ = Opportunities are around   ⊖ = Be on the defensive   ⬤ = Life is pretty ordinary

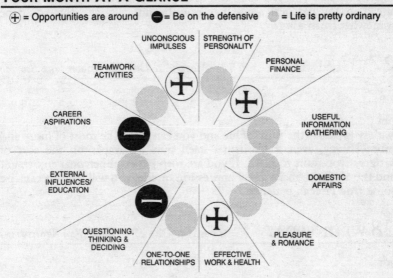

JANUARY HIGHS AND LOWS

Here I show you how the rhythms of the Moon will affect you this month. Like the tide, your energies and abilities will rise and fall with its pattern. When it is above the centre line, go for it, when it is below, you should be resting.

HIGH 4TH–5TH   **HIGH** 31ST

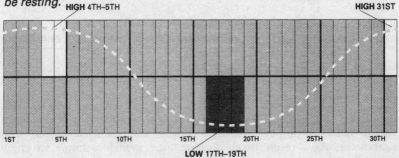

LOW 17TH–19TH

39

26 MONDAY
Moon Age Day 25   Moon Sign Scorpio

am . . . .

pm . . . .
It could become quite clear that a change in attitude is necessary when it comes to personal attachments. Maybe your partner is behaving in a slightly odd way and it's up to you to discover why this might be. Getting ahead in any practical sense may now be difficult, and this could be somewhat frustrating.

27 TUESDAY
Moon Age Day 26   Moon Sign Scorpio

am . . . .

pm . . . .
Variety is clearly the spice of life and you can make the most of more and more energy, even if Christmas itself puts a damper on the sort of progress you want to make. If you are torn between personal enjoyment and the ability to make a real impression on life, you will have to exercise some true Piscean patience.

28 WEDNESDAY
Moon Age Day 27   Moon Sign Sagittarius

am . . . .

pm . . . .
Mentally speaking you remain potentially restless and might decide to ring the changes to avoid becoming frustrated. You could join forces with those around you who are feeling equally dynamic in order to make the best impression you can on the world at large. Finances could begin to look stronger than you imagined.

29 THURSDAY
Moon Age Day 28   Moon Sign Sagittarius

am . . . .

pm . . . .
You can make this a fairly brisk time socially and you may well discover that some of the recent frustrations are now disappearing. Confidence should still be strong but you are willing to suspend some actions until next week. As a result there is more time available simply to enjoy yourself in the company of family and friends.

30 FRIDAY

Moon Age Day 0   Moon Sign Capricorn

am . . . .

pm . . . .
This is a time during which the results of past practical efforts may well make themselves felt. Don't get too tied up with details because it is clearly the overall picture that is important at present. A job you have been involved with for quite some time could be nearly over.

31 SATURDAY

Moon Age Day 1   Moon Sign Capricorn

am . . . .

pm . . . .
At the very end of the year your love life might prove to be slightly problematic. Although this reminds you that you have to show that extra bit of concern and love, it shouldn't be a lasting situation. With a recognition of the needs of those around you, it is possible to have everything fully on course for a splendid evening.

1 SUNDAY

Moon Age Day 2   Moon Sign Aquarius

am . . . .

pm . . . .
A quieter day is possible, with plenty available to keep you busy but a need for some solitude. You have what it takes to make a good impression but might decide to keep your sights limited to people you already know. You can use today to sort out your ideas not only for the new week that lies ahead but also for a whole new year!

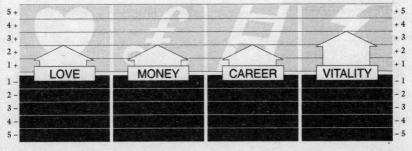

2 MONDAY
Moon Age Day 3   Moon Sign Aquarius

am ....

pm ....
The emphasis now shifts to social fun and you should have little or no trouble putting yourself in precisely the right company at just the right time. There are quieter moments on offer too, because the Moon is entering your solar twelfth house, but in the main you can afford to seek out a good time, most likely with friends.

3 TUESDAY
Moon Age Day 4   Moon Sign Aquarius

am ....

pm ....
Beware of taking situations for granted today. You need to think things through and probably won't be in the best frame of mind for doing anything particularly outrageous. In the main you may decide to stick to what you know, and might also opt to fall in line with the plans and opinions of those around you.

4 WEDNESDAY
Moon Age Day 5   Moon Sign Pisces

am ....

pm ....
Confidence has potential to be on the increase. This is the time of the month that the Moon occupies your own zodiac sign, a period known as the lunar high. You have what it takes to make positive decisions and to fight for your right to please yourself. Romance could also be on the cards under present influences.

5 THURSDAY
Moon Age Day 6   Moon Sign Pisces

am ....

pm ....
It's time to see what Lady Luck can do for you. Be willing to take a chance today, because to do so is likely to lead to greater success. You have scope to convince others to follow your lead, and though the position of leader of the pack isn't one that Pisces would normally choose, you could well do so now.

6 FRIDAY
Moon Age Day 7   Moon Sign Aries

am ....

pm ....
A gradual shift to a better financial position seems possible, starting today. You can be wise in your judgements and shouldn't be taking unnecessary chances. At the same time you know a bargain when you see one and should be in a good position to maximise any cash that is available.

7 SATURDAY
Moon Age Day 8   Moon Sign Aries

am ....

pm ....
This is not a time to speculate too much when it comes to important decisions. Although you might be good with cash at the moment, you may not be quite so lucky when it comes to sorting out relationships or the more practical aspects of your life. There may be people around whose advice you are now quite willing to take.

8 SUNDAY
Moon Age Day 9   Moon Sign Taurus

am ....

pm ....
During the present time you are inclined to look for convivial surroundings and an easy-going atmosphere. You probably won't want to be sorting out the arguments of others and nor would you presently be willing to dump your own ideas at the whim of friends. Taken all in all, Pisces can be awkward now, but understandably so.

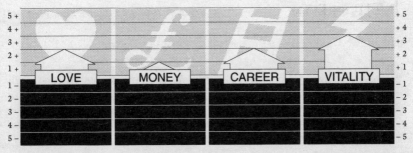

9 MONDAY

Moon Age Day 10   Moon Sign Taurus

am . . . .

pm . . . .
You can take advantage of a great deal happening in friendship at the beginning of a new working week, so much in fact that you may not have as much time to concentrate on the practical matters of life as you might wish. Your best response is not to try to do everything at once, and to leave some of the decisions to others.

10 TUESDAY

Moon Age Day 11   Moon Sign Gemini

am . . . .

pm . . . .
The Moon is now in your solar fourth house, a position that encourages a homely frame of mind. You may well be happy to stay in amongst your family members and to do all you can to please your partner. Even if not everyone is on your side at the moment, any awkward people you encounter probably don't really matter to your life.

11 WEDNESDAY

Moon Age Day 12   Moon Sign Gemini

am . . . .

pm . . . .
Whilst your mind tends to be working overtime at the moment, it may be all you can do to keep up physically. It is possible that you might tire more easily than normal, since you don't have quite the planetary support to move mountains. There are ways round everything, for example, allowing your friends to take some of the strain.

12 THURSDAY

Moon Age Day 13   Moon Sign Gemini

am . . . .

pm . . . .
Your ego is presently reflected in the way you are able to deal with relationships, especially romantic ones. For once you can believe in yourself fully and when you are in this frame of mind you appear even more attractive than usual. There are some slight financial gains to be made, but outright gambling is probably unwise.

13 FRIDAY
Moon Age Day 14   Moon Sign Cancer

am . . . .

pm . . . .
Mars is now in your solar third house, suggesting you may be rather more hot tempered than is usually the case for the zodiac sign of Pisces. This fact might surprise others, particularly if you are usually quite mild in your attitude. It doesn't do people any harm to have their preconceptions shattered once in a while.

14 SATURDAY
Moon Age Day 15   Moon Sign Cancer

am . . . .

pm . . . .
Now is the time to take advantage of social invitations, which makes for a crackerjack of a weekend for many Pisces subjects. There are times when you needn't wait to be asked but can make the running yourself. Someone could be very surprised when they see you pushing yourself forward in this way.

15 SUNDAY
Moon Age Day 16   Moon Sign Leo

am . . . .

pm . . . .
Better work prospects around now offer the opportunity to move closer towards personal targets, though of course this trend is less evident if Sunday is a day of rest for you. By all means plan for tomorrow and in the meantime if an interesting personal or social offer comes along, put on your best clothes and have a good time.

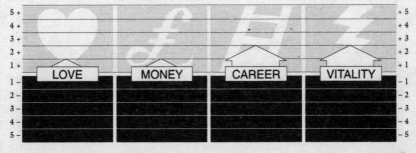

16 MONDAY
Moon Age Day 17   Moon Sign Leo

am . . . .

pm . . . .
You have scope to keep up a varied social life this week, and there is just
a possibility that other responsibilities, such as work for example, might
get in the way of you doing so. Look towards a particular objective,
because every small step you take in the right direction helps to lead you
to your ultimate goal.

17 TUESDAY
Moon Age Day 18   Moon Sign Virgo

am . . . .

pm . . . .
Don't make life difficult for yourself by being too emotional. The Moon
is in your opposite zodiac sign, that part of the month known as the lunar
low. You may not have quite the level of energy you would wish, and you
could be slightly grumpier than usual. It is still important to focus your
mind carefully.

18 WEDNESDAY
Moon Age Day 19   Moon Sign Virgo

am . . . .

pm . . . .
This is not the time to be tempting fate with risky ventures. At the same
time you could have just a little trouble in expressing yourself in the way
you would wish. Instead of trying to push ahead today, why not take time
out to think about life and to watch others accomplishing things?

19 THURSDAY
Moon Age Day 20   Moon Sign Virgo

am . . . .

pm . . . .
As the lunar low begins to move away, you can ensure your social life
starts to take a turn for the better. You can strike up new and important
friendships, whilst old attachments take on a different sort of feel. Where
romance is concerned, you could be in the right frame of mind to sweep
someone off their feet.

20 FRIDAY

Moon Age Day 21   Moon Sign Libra

am . . . .

pm . . . .
A great deal of enthusiasm can be put into communication and social interactions today. You have what it takes to make yourself the centre of attraction and that can be of particular help to you in a professional sense. This is the time to dust off a few of your more grandiose ideas and to introduce them to the world.

21 SATURDAY

Moon Age Day 22   Moon Sign Libra

am . . . .

pm . . . .
It's possible that not everyone you meet at the moment is to be trusted, and you need to be careful not to place too much reliance on what you are being told. If you use your intuition, which is always your best ally, you are less likely to go wrong. You can afford to devote some of your time to family matters later in the day.

22 SUNDAY

Moon Age Day 23   Moon Sign Scorpio

am . . . .

pm . . . .
The present position of the Moon temporarily offers a boost to all aspects related to travel. As a result you might choose to get out of the house today and to go somewhere you find particularly interesting. Even if the weather is not very good, your desire for fresh fields and pastures new is probably strong.

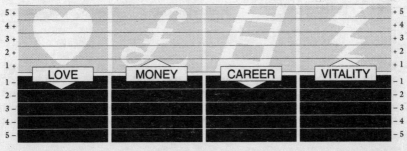

23 MONDAY
Moon Age Day 24   Moon Sign Scorpio

am . . . .

pm . . . .
Concentrating on the job at hand might not be very easy. Mercury is in your solar twelfth house, a planetary position that can distract you quite a lot. At the same time there is no doubt that your intuition is especially strong, and you have the ability to look past what people are saying, straight into the heart of what they really mean.

24 TUESDAY
Moon Age Day 25   Moon Sign Scorpio

am . . . .

pm . . . .
This is a wonderful time for friendships and for getting people on your side. You can allow the naturally charming side of your nature to shine out like a beacon, so that practically everyone wants to be your friend. It is difficult to dislike Pisceans, and the way you are behaving at the moment it is almost impossible!

25 WEDNESDAY
Moon Age Day 26   Moon Sign Sagittarius

am . . . .

pm . . . .
Projecting your thoughts and wishes could be easier now than at any time for the last few months. If there are certain things you want to do that require the co-operation of others, you can use the sheer force of your magnetic personality to get the help you need. Don't be shy when in the company of strangers.

26 THURSDAY
Moon Age Day 27   Moon Sign Sagittarius

am . . . .

pm . . . .
If you are uncertain today about your goals and objectives, taking some time out would be no bad thing. Pisces always needs quiet interludes and a good deal of meditation. Today works better if you take life one step at a time and if you avoid getting involved in situations you either don't understand or simply dislike.

27 FRIDAY
Moon Age Day 28   Moon Sign Capricorn

am . . . .

pm . . . .
This is potentially the best time of the month to get out and meet new
people. The present position of Venus in your solar chart means that your
friendliness is well accented. Expressing yourself might also be simpler
than is sometimes the case for such a complex individual as you.

28 SATURDAY
Moon Age Day 29   Moon Sign Capricorn

am . . . .

pm . . . .
The influences are favourable for social ambitions this weekend, and all
group activities are especially well highlighted under present planetary
trends. You are able to offer significant help and support to those who
need it. Even if you don't know the people concerned, you have what it
takes to lend a hand.

29 SUNDAY
Moon Age Day 0   Moon Sign Aquarius

am . . . .

pm . . . .
Compassion is your middle name, and particularly so today. By helping
others, you invariably do yourself some good too, though of course that
is not why you offer assistance. Modest and unassuming, you have the
power to create a groundswell of affection coming at you from many of
the people you meet today.

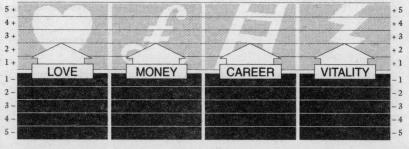

30 MONDAY
Moon Age Day 1   Moon Sign Aquarius

am ....

pm ....
This is not the best day of the month for clear-headed planning. The fact is that with the Moon in your solar twelfth house, you could become quite muddled. Your best approach is to avoid taking major decisions now, and allow others to make most of the running. You may well decide to stay close to home.

31 TUESDAY
Moon Age Day 2   Moon Sign Pisces

am ....

pm ....
The lunar high is with you again, allowing you to blow away all the dust in your brain on a wind of change and enthusiasm. With everything to play for, you can end January on the best note possible. You know what you want from life and what is more important, you are probably sure how to go about getting it.

1 WEDNESDAY
Moon Age Day 3   Moon Sign Pisces

am ....

pm ....
This is an excellent time for putting new ideas into practice and for enlisting the support of people who are higher up the tree than you are. All ambitions tend to crowd in whilst you are in such a dynamic frame of mind, and there isn't much doubt about your commitment to anything that takes your fancy.

2 THURSDAY
Moon Age Day 4   Moon Sign Aries

am ....

pm ....
Trends suggest you may now have a quite unworldly angle on personal matters, which is characterised by selflessness and high ideals. That's fine, but the world won't always match up to your expectations of it. You can't help being the sort of person you are, but your natural sensitivity can sometimes lead to disappointment.

50

3 FRIDAY

Moon Age Day 5   Moon Sign Aries

am . . . .

pm . . . .
You tend to take a slightly more passive role in life today, especially in contrast to the situation earlier in the week. You should be willing to go with the flow under all but the most important circumstances, and you are also able to adapt your nature to suit those of the people with whom you interact.

4 SATURDAY

Moon Age Day 6   Moon Sign Taurus

am . . . .

pm . . . .
Communications at this time may well involve tension or ego on the part of others. Adapting yourself to this state of affairs shouldn't be difficult, but it might become tiring having to play a defensive role. The answer is simple – take yourself away from the offending people for an hour or two and do something that pleases you.

5 SUNDAY

Moon Age Day 7   Moon Sign Taurus

am . . . .

pm . . . .
You need to keep a strong element of variety in your life around now and needn't be too willing to stick to the same old Sunday routines. Not only can you please yourself by bringing a little change into your day, but you can ensure others are happy too. Not everyone you meet is going to be pleasant, but don't worry – that's life!

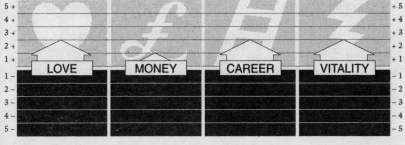

February 2006

YOUR MONTH AT A GLANCE

⊕ = Opportunities are around   ⊖ = Be on the defensive   ◯ = Life is pretty ordinary

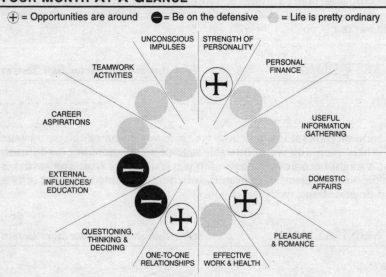

FEBRUARY HIGHS AND LOWS

Here I show you how the rhythms of the Moon will affect you this month. Like the tide, your energies and abilities will rise and fall with its pattern. When it is above the centre line, go for it, when it is below, you should be resting.

HIGH 1ST   HIGH 27TH–28TH

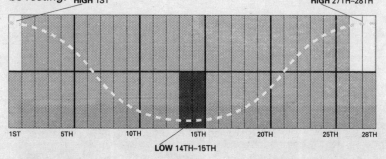

1ST   5TH   10TH   15TH   20TH   25TH   28TH

LOW 14TH–15TH

6 MONDAY
Moon Age Day 8   Moon Sign Gemini

am . . . .

pm . . . .
The potential for a much improved social life gets better and better.
Venus can really help you at the moment and allows you to make that
special impression that makes all the difference. Almost nobody will be
immune to your charms at present and you can afford to seek out some
interesting people.

7 TUESDAY
Moon Age Day 9   Moon Sign Gemini

am . . . .

pm . . . .
This may prove to be a very busy period at home and a time during which
you are able to offer a good deal of support to loved ones. As far as the
practicalities of life are concerned, you manage to address these with very
little trouble. Getting colleagues onside might well bring one or two
small problems.

8 WEDNESDAY
Moon Age Day 10   Moon Sign Gemini

am . . . .

pm . . . .
You might be inclined to let others have a very powerful effect on you as
far as your personal life is concerned. It is possible that you are listening
to too much gossip, or else someone is deliberately trying to mislead you.
The important thing is to decide for yourself, based on evidence that is
in front of your eyes.

9 THURSDAY
Moon Age Day 11   Moon Sign Cancer

am . . . .

pm . . . .
Even if the emotional influences surrounding you at the moment are not
in any way heavy, you could still be too sensitive in some ways. Try to
keep it light and breezy today and mix as freely as you can with the sort
of people who fire your imagination and your sense of fun.

53

10 FRIDAY

Moon Age Day 12   Moon Sign Cancer

am . . . .

pm . . . .
Trends encourage you down the path of original thinking today and
that's no bad thing. In some ways you might also be turning detective,
particularly if there are any little mysteries around that you are keen to
solve. Pisces can show its usual sensitivity when you are dealing with
people who have problems in their lives.

11 SATURDAY

Moon Age Day 13   Moon Sign Leo

am . . . .

pm . . . .
Where work is concerned it is possible that you will have to pace yourself
today, and this doesn't simply apply to your professional life. When it
comes to getting chores done around the house you may decide to take
your time, but you can also sort things out much better if you enlist a
little practical help.

12 SUNDAY

Moon Age Day 14   Moon Sign Leo

am . . . .

pm . . . .
You could feel rather uninspired or even confused under present
planetary trends. It is important to realise that when you don't know
something, you might find someone around who does. The time is right
to rely on what others tell you and not to be frightened to ask one or two
leading questions if it is necessary.

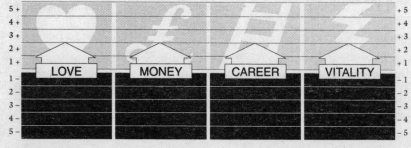

13 MONDAY   *Moon Age Day 15   Moon Sign Leo*

am . . . .

pm . . . .
Beware of unnecessary distractions at the beginning of this working
week. Mars is presently in your solar third house, which can indicate
possible confusion. Taken together with the slightly deteriorating
position of the Moon in your solar chart, you may decide to opt for a
fairly quiet time for the next couple of days.

14 TUESDAY   *Moon Age Day 16   Moon Sign Virgo*

am . . . .

pm . . . .
The lunar low may seem to sap your strength and prevent you from
getting on quite as well as you might wish. Life could throw up
challenges that look interesting, but this isn't the right time to be taking
risks of any sort. Treat setbacks with a shrug of your shoulders and a smile
because they should only be temporary.

15 WEDNESDAY   *Moon Age Day 17   Moon Sign Virgo*

am . . . .

pm . . . .
This is one of the times during the month when it might be far better to
allow your partner or family members to take some of the decisions. If
you are not seeing things quite as clearly as would normally be the case,
you might blunder into problems without realising you are doing so.

16 THURSDAY   *Moon Age Day 18   Moon Sign Libra*

am . . . .

pm . . . .
There are signs that strong feelings have a large role to play between
yourself and someone else – most probably at work. You can certainly
afford to be a good deal more definite in a general sense and the social
prospects are also better now. Don't get agitated if things don't always
seem to go your way.

17 FRIDAY
Moon Age Day 19   Moon Sign Libra

am . . . .

pm . . . .
There shouldn't be too much need to put yourself out wholesale on behalf of others. It appears that you can't avoid being helpful, and in any case there may be individuals around at the moment who want to treat you. You have scope to improve your emotional responses and to make the most of original ideas.

18 SATURDAY
Moon Age Day 20   Moon Sign Libra

am . . . .

pm . . . .
You seem able to dominate your domestic surroundings at present, which is probably no bad thing now that the weekend has arrived. Any difficulties that might come into the lives of those you love can be dealt with efficiently and originally by your typical Piscean temperament. Your partner may well be in a very funny frame of mind.

19 SUNDAY
Moon Age Day 21   Moon Sign Scorpio

am . . . .

pm . . . .
The present position of the Moon allows you to bring out the gypsy in your soul. If you have a yearning for new horizons, you may well decide that this would be a good day on which to take a trip of some sort. It doesn't really matter how far you go because it is simply the change that is important.

20 MONDAY   *Moon Age Day 22   Moon Sign Scorpio*

am . . . .

pm . . . .
A period of significant optimism is now on offer. The Sun is entering your solar first house, where it remains for the next month or so. It should be much easier to make life work the way you would wish, whilst at the same time you will notice just how much more responsive you can persuade other people to be.

21 TUESDAY   *Moon Age Day 23   Moon Sign Sagittarius*

am . . . .

pm . . . .
Professionally speaking, working Pisces individuals could now be feeling rather more secure. Of course it isn't given to you to be over-confident, but you can gain assistance and reassurance from those you work with. When it comes to out-of-work activities, why not look for opportunties to try something new?

22 WEDNESDAY   *Moon Age Day 24   Moon Sign Sagittarius*

am . . . .

pm . . . .
There is great potential for new friendships to start at any time now. Pisces generally keeps its friends, often for life, but you do need new stimulus now and again, and that is what is on offer at present. Don't turn down the chance for an exciting encounter with someone you hold in high regard.

23 THURSDAY   *Moon Age Day 25   Moon Sign Capricorn*

am . . . .

pm . . . .
The Sun now enhances your leadership qualities and your ability to make your instructions to others concise and impossible to misunderstand. You might not always think of yourself as a leader, but your winning ways and warm personality make people quite happy to do what you think is best.

24 FRIDAY
Moon Age Day 26   Moon Sign Capricorn

am . . . .

pm . . . .
You should avoid trying to manipulate others at home, whilst at the same time keeping an eye on them. It's a fine line to walk, but if anyone can achieve it, you can. Beware of getting involved in power games, either at work or at home. You have your own way of getting to where you need to be and you are not a bulldozer!

25 SATURDAY
Moon Age Day 27   Moon Sign Aquarius

am . . . .

pm . . . .
Social relationships now have a much better foundation than might have been the case earlier in the month, offering scope for you to get on very well with those around you. The shyness that sometimes typifies your zodiac sign seems to be taking a holiday, and you can afford to be more 'up-front' than ever.

26 SUNDAY
Moon Age Day 28   Moon Sign Aquarius

am . . . .

pm . . . .
Plans become more important as the weekend brings more exciting trends along. You take genuine pleasure in anything new or unusual and tend to be more intrepid than might sometimes be the case. You may decide to seek out people who have a very unusual and refreshing view of life.

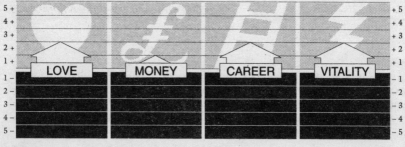

27 MONDAY

Moon Age Day 29   Moon Sign Pisces

am . . . .

pm . . . .

As the end of the month beckons, so you come to the most dynamic phase of February. The Moon is in your zodiac sign, and the Sun remains in your solar first house. It's all go and you will need all that renewed energy just to keep up with the possibilities. You needn't let anyone decide anything for you today.

28 TUESDAY

Moon Age Day 0   Moon Sign Pisces

am . . . .

pm . . . .

Have faith in yourself and in what you have decided to do. You can achieve almost anything you wish right now, not simply because you have energy, but because you can work things out so carefully. You can even afford to take a chance or two, whilst at the same time playing the percentage game like a professional.

1 WEDNESDAY

Moon Age Day 1   Moon Sign Aries

am . . . .

pm . . . .

Just the right sort of influences are present today and they come courtesy of one of the best planetary line-ups for ages as far as you are concerned. Your intuition is especially strong and shouldn't let you down when it comes to making decisions. You can also use these trends to make improvements in your personal life.

2 THURSDAY   ☿

Moon Age Day 2   Moon Sign Aries

am . . . .

pm . . . .

You could find that you are encountering minor problems when it comes to people at home. Perhaps not everyone to whom you are related thinks you are the bee's knees at present, and this may be especially true in the case of younger people. Just use your usual Piscean patience and you can make everything come good.

3 FRIDAY ☿ *Moon Age Day 3   Moon Sign Taurus*

am ....

pm ....
Even if there is turmoil in your life today, you can match it with your ability to deal with matters as and when they come along. Too much prior planning may be difficult, if not impossible, and you need to keep your eye on the ball. Personal attachments can be strengthened as the day unfolds.

4 SATURDAY ☿ *Moon Age Day 4   Moon Sign Taurus*

am ....

pm ....
You have scope to make yourself very attractive to others at the moment, and they could be gathering round you for several different reasons. Most importantly, you seem to know what you are doing, which others may not. By the end of the day you may decide that a social outing is what you want – but plan it earlier if you can.

5 SUNDAY ☿ *Moon Age Day 5   Moon Sign Gemini*

am ....

pm ....
You should still be confident and will probably be achieving a physical peak in terms of energy. With everything to play for, you can make this a Sunday to remember. When it comes to the influence you have over others, you seem to be on especially good form, so now is the time to ask for what you really want.

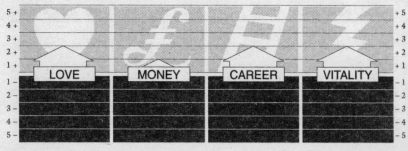

March 2006

YOUR MONTH AT A GLANCE

$\oplus$ = Opportunities are around $\ominus$ = Be on the defensive   ● = Life is pretty ordinary

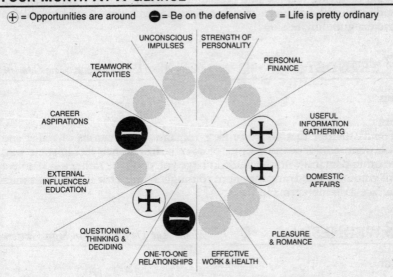

UNCONSCIOUS IMPULSES
STRENGTH OF PERSONALITY
TEAMWORK ACTIVITIES
PERSONAL FINANCE
CAREER ASPIRATIONS
USEFUL INFORMATION GATHERING
EXTERNAL INFLUENCES/ EDUCATION
DOMESTIC AFFAIRS
QUESTIONING, THINKING & DECIDING
ONE-TO-ONE RELATIONSHIPS
EFFECTIVE WORK & HEALTH
PLEASURE & ROMANCE

MARCH HIGHS AND LOWS

Here I show you how the rhythms of the Moon will affect you this month. Like the tide, your energies and abilities will rise and fall with its pattern. When it is above the centre line, go for it, when it is below, you should be resting.

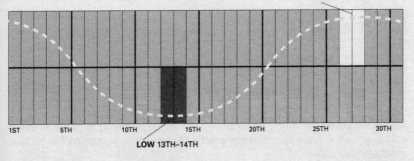

HIGH 27TH–28TH

1ST   5TH   10TH   15TH   20TH   25TH   30TH

LOW 13TH–14TH

61

6 MONDAY ☿ *Moon Age Day 6   Moon Sign Gemini*

am . . . .

pm . . . .
The main emphasis for today seems to be on family matters, and the way you deal with them is quite important. Younger people in particular could be giving you the odd problem, but yours is a very understanding zodiac sign and you can use that now. At work you should be able to make a good impression.

7 TUESDAY ☿ *Moon Age Day 7   Moon Sign Gemini*

am . . . .

pm . . . .
Trends suggest that you may have romantic expectations of today and will want to sweep your partner or sweetheart off their feet in some way. In other contacts with the world at large you could be rather too sensitive for your own good, and may need to toughen up a little if you don't want to face a disappointment.

8 WEDNESDAY ☿ *Moon Age Day 8   Moon Sign Cancer*

am . . . .

pm . . . .
The Sun remains in your solar first house, offering energy and confidence in the main. Although you have what it takes to get ahead, you can be held up because of your constant concern for others. By all means try to offload just a few of the responsibilities, especially those which are not yours in the first place.

9 THURSDAY ☿ *Moon Age Day 9   Moon Sign Cancer*

am . . . .

pm . . . .
You should get a lot of fun today from the fact that you can widen your social circle considerably. It would be sensible to make sure you achieve an early start to the day. That way you can get chores out of the way early and leave time later for relaxing a little. Confidence seems to be on the increase generally.

10 FRIDAY ☿ *Moon Age Day 10   Moon Sign Leo*

am . . . .

pm . . . .
Even if family needs once again take priority today, you can find time to mix with your friends, which is quite important at the moment. Be careful that you don't step on the toes of anyone who has real influence in your professional life. Your usual diplomatic approach to situations now works best.

11 SATURDAY ☿ *Moon Age Day 11   Moon Sign Leo*

am . . . .

pm . . . .
You may not get your own way as much today as you would wish, and might have to forego certain pleasures that you usually take for granted. Routines can be a bit of a bore and it is worth putting extra energy into jobs now so that they don't come back to haunt you later. Stopgap measures won't do.

12 SUNDAY ☿ *Moon Age Day 12   Moon Sign Leo*

am . . . .

pm . . . .
A potentially better day, and one that can lead to big ideas. Try to get some adventure into your life and leave aside some of the less important tasks today in favour of enjoying yourself. Everyone is entitled to have some time to themselves and today is ripe for fun and games. Why not persuade friends to join in?

63

13 MONDAY ☿ *Moon Age Day 13   Moon Sign Virgo*

am . . . .

pm . . . .
There are some setbacks possible, influenced in the main by the arrival of
the lunar low. Your best approach is to show a bit of patience and wait
for things to look better. It isn't as if anything major should go wrong,
in fact you might come to realise that when you are worrying, you are
doing so about nothing.

14 TUESDAY ☿ *Moon Age Day 14   Moon Sign Virgo*

am . . . .

pm . . . .
A fairly sluggish period is indicated, but there is room for that bit of
individual effort that can make all the difference. By the evening you
should find that some of your energy is returning, and even if you still
don't want to push over any buses, you may decide to get out of the
house in the company of friends.

15 WEDNESDAY ☿ *Moon Age Day 15   Moon Sign Libra*

am . . . .

pm . . . .
Avoid being heavy-handed in your dealings with family members. It
might be best to stay away from family issues for the moment, in favour
of spending as much time as you can amongst friends. If not everyone to
whom you are related is on the same wavelength as you are right now,
that could be where the problems start.

16 THURSDAY ☿ *Moon Age Day 16   Moon Sign Libra*

am . . . .

pm . . . .
Matters of love and affection are presently tempered by practical
considerations. You probably have to respond to some of the more
material matters that demand your attention, and that means having to
shelve your personal feelings just a little. You should find time later in the
day to redress the balance a little.

17 FRIDAY   ☿   *Moon Age Day 17   Moon Sign Libra*

am . . . .

pm . . . .
Your sense of self-determination has rarely looked better than it does at
the moment. Most Pisceans can now afford to be very single-minded,
and few people will argue with your point of view if they recognise the
power you are generating. You shouldn't have to shout at anyone to get
what you want at present – a simple look should do.

18 SATURDAY   ☿   *Moon Age Day 18   Moon Sign Scorpio*

am . . . .

pm . . . .
In discussions of any sort you are able to express yourself well. This
doesn't mean you are browbeating anyone, simply that the magnetic
quality of your personality is extremely strong. This would be a good
period for travel or for indulging in any form of cultural matter that takes
your fancy.

19 SUNDAY   ☿   *Moon Age Day 19   Moon Sign Scorpio*

am . . . .

pm . . . .
In current relationships it is a fact that your head has to rule your heart
today. Venus is in your solar twelfth house so there are some limitations
placed upon romance, but don't assume that personal attachments are
everything. On the contrary, you can also get great fun out of being with
your friends, especially in the evening.

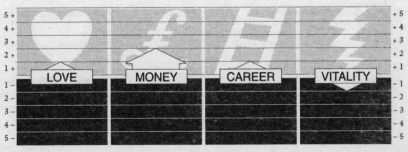

20 MONDAY ☿ *Moon Age Day 20* *Moon Sign Sagittarius*

am . . . .

pm . . . .
As the Sun is about to leave your solar first house, you would be wise to take the final crucial step today towards an objective that is very important to you. You can get ahead quite easily, especially at work. It isn't out of the question that advancement of some sort will be within your reach before today is out.

21 TUESDAY ☿ *Moon Age Day 21* *Moon Sign Sagittarius*

am . . . .

pm . . . .
The Sun moves into your solar second house today, which could prove to be quite useful in terms of finances. Now is a good time to get new money flowing into your life, and there might be more of it about than you had been expecting. Great success is possible, but it requires an extra input of effort on your part.

22 WEDNESDAY ☿ *Moon Age Day 22* *Moon Sign Sagittarius*

am . . . .

pm . . . .
At work you should now strive to do your very best. Success is on offer just around every potential corner and there isn't much doubt that you are keen to get ahead at the moment. Although this area of your life is important, it shouldn't be allowed to get in the way of deeper and more personal aspects.

23 THURSDAY ☿ *Moon Age Day 23* *Moon Sign Capricorn*

am . . . .

pm . . . .
Trends assist you to win friends and influence people with very little effort at the moment. Pisces is at its influential best and you only have to speak to get what you want. This is fine but doesn't answer the more personal questions you are asking yourself at present. It might be time for a heart-to-heart with someone who is very important to you.

24 FRIDAY
 Moon Age Day 24   Moon Sign Capricorn

am ....

pm ....
Whilst you are at work today it is best to give yourself fully to any new situations and fresh starts that are showing themselves. However, you would be wise to compartment your day and should be willing to leave work behind once the evening arrives. You can afford to put down anything that stops you from simply relaxing.

25 SATURDAY
☿ *Moon Age Day 25   Moon Sign Aquarius*

am ....

pm ....
With Mercury in your solar first house your mental powers are highlighted. Solving problems might be easy, though getting others to keep up with your way of thinking might be slightly more difficult. You seem to need to explain yourself time and again, which could be slightly wearing to other people.

26 SUNDAY
Moon Age Day 26   Moon Sign Aquarius

am ....

pm ....
You could be in for a slightly quieter period whilst the Moon passes through your solar twelfth house. As a result you might be more reflective today and less likely to excel in the way you have of late. This needn't be too much of a problem on a Sunday, when you can enjoy the chance to be quiet.

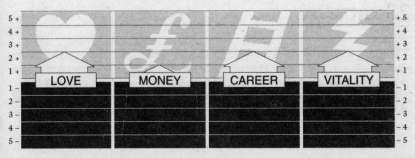

27 MONDAY
Moon Age Day 27   Moon Sign Pisces

am . . . .

pm . . . .
Certain of the life choices you make now could well have great implications later on, though this needn't prevent you from taking chances today. The lunar high sees you raring to go and anxious to make the very best sort of impression when it counts the most. A day to ditch pointless routines and go for gold, no matter what you are doing!

28 TUESDAY
Moon Age Day 28   Moon Sign Pisces

am . . . .

pm . . . .
You need to be in the running for a good time and should not allow little distractions to get in the way. Getting on with a dozen different things at the same time shouldn't be too much of a problem, and you have what it takes to make the best possible impression on the world as a whole.

29 WEDNESDAY
Moon Age Day 0   Moon Sign Aries

am . . . .

pm . . . .
You can make the best use of financial advantages around this time. You can afford to trust your intuition when dealing with others and to offer the sort of advice that Pisceans find easy to give. Your concern for others is one of the reasons why you can now attract so much attention.

30 THURSDAY
Moon Age Day 1   Moon Sign Aries

am . . . .

pm . . . .
Venus is still in your solar twelfth house and this could prove to be something of a setback. This is not the best of times to be making new plans and it is important to consolidate your position before you move forward in any way. In particular, beware of taking chances with solid personal relationships.

31 FRIDAY   *Moon Age Day 2   Moon Sign Taurus*

am . . . .

pm . . . .
Original ideas and insights today can be used to advance your plans no
end and you need to listen carefully to that little voice inside your head.
You can get useful feedback from colleagues and friends, whilst at the
same time responding to that very strong intuition. Almost everything is
in the balance today.

1 SATURDAY   *Moon Age Day 3   Moon Sign Taurus*

am . . . .

pm . . . .
It's the start of a new month, and you have scope to put the pursuit of
money high on your agenda as April gets started. You would be wise to
keep a careful eye on your personal budget and might have to take family
members to task if you think they are spending too freely. A day to use
your diplomacy and avoid arguments.

2 SUNDAY   *Moon Age Day 4   Moon Sign Gemini*

am . . . .

pm . . . .
Emotions can be strong today and you can make this one of the best days
of the month for personal attachments. Finding the right words to tell
someone how important they are to you shouldn't be difficult and this is
the sort of day during which you can make the most of some unexpected
but exciting invitations.

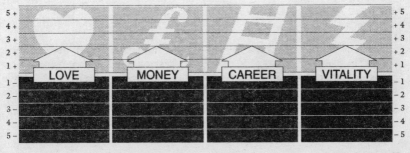

April 2006

YOUR MONTH AT A GLANCE

⊕ = Opportunities are around   ⊖ = Be on the defensive   ◯ = Life is pretty ordinary

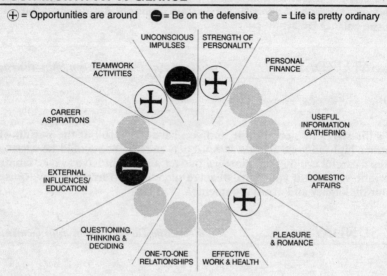

APRIL HIGHS AND LOWS

Here I show you how the rhythms of the Moon will affect you this month. Like the tide, your energies and abilities will rise and fall with its pattern. When it is above the centre line, go for it, when it is below, you should be resting.

HIGH 23RD–24TH

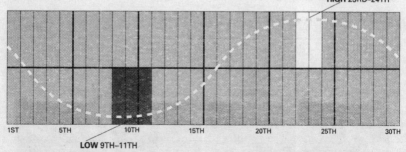

1ST   5TH   10TH   15TH   20TH   25TH   30TH

LOW 9TH–11TH

3 MONDAY
Moon Age Day 5   Moon Sign Gemini

am . . . .

pm . . . .
You might have to re-evaluate your attitude towards something in the domestic arena, though home life generally should more than compensate for any lack of achievements in other areas of your life as this week gets started. Younger family members in particular can be a source of joy under present influences.

4 TUESDAY
Moon Age Day 6   Moon Sign Cancer

am . . . .

pm . . . .
Good financial prospects seem to prevail under present trends and even if you aren't exactly rolling in money at the moment, you have scope to come up with some good ideas for getting more cash. Not everyone is likely to be on your side at work, but you probably have more influence than you think.

5 WEDNESDAY
Moon Age Day 7   Moon Sign Cancer

am . . . .

pm . . . .
Take full advantage of all that is happening within your social and romantic life at this stage. There are some significant gains on offer and you should get on especially well with other Water-sign people. These are Cancerians, Scorpios and other Pisceans. The most casual of chats could help you to recognise some far-reaching implications.

6 THURSDAY
Moon Age Day 8   Moon Sign Cancer

am . . . .

pm . . . .
Even if domestic matters are now prone to a few disruptions, you needn't let these bother you unduly. The problem, if it can be called that, is influenced by the present position of the Moon. You should avoid getting bogged down by pointless discussions or changes in your routines that prove unhelpful.

7 FRIDAY
Moon Age Day 9   Moon Sign Leo

am . . . .

pm . . . .
This is a time during which you can make romantic matters look very
lively. Venus has now moved into your solar first house, helping you to
elicit a warm response from other people. It is possible that you will
discover admirers you didn't know you had, thought the revelation could
prove to be a little embarrassing.

8 SATURDAY
Moon Age Day 10   Moon Sign Leo

am . . . .

pm . . . .
You should feel happy to be useful today and can be of particular benefit
to both family members and friends. You might not feel inclined to do a
lot in the way of work, but there are advantages to relaxing at the
moment. Social trends look especially good, particularly for the evening.

9 SUNDAY
Moon Age Day 11   Moon Sign Virgo

am . . . .

pm . . . .
This is hardly the best time of the month for taking risks of any sort, and
you would be well advised to keep a fairly low profile if you can. Not
everyone seems to agree with your point of view, and there is no point at
all in falling out with anyone if you can avoid doing so. The lunar low has
potential to sap your resolve.

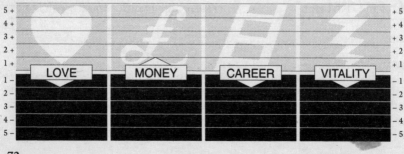

10 MONDAY   *Moon Age Day 12   Moon Sign Virgo*

am . . . .

pm . . . .
Progress could be decidedly difficult, but you need to tell yourself that you cannot be pushing ahead all the time. Your best response is to take stock of some situations and clear the decks for actions you know are going to come soon. A day to get some rest and, if possible, to get involved in new hobbies or pastimes.

11 TUESDAY   *Moon Age Day 13   Moon Sign Virgo*

am . . . .

pm . . . .
Domestic matters may not be very smooth with Mars in your solar fourth house. There are signs that you could be a little touchy with relatives, whose responses to you might not be all that wonderful either. As a result you may decide to spend more time with friends and less hours at home.

12 WEDNESDAY   *Moon Age Day 14   Moon Sign Libra*

am . . . .

pm . . . .
You might have to deal with some fairly difficult emotional matters around now – at least before you get out to enjoy yourself. Matters associated with finance could also cause you a few problems, though there probably isn't any real reason why this should be the case. Perhaps you are just in an agitated frame of mind.

13 THURSDAY   *Moon Age Day 15   Moon Sign Libra*

am . . . .

pm . . . .
Any new ideas that you put to the test today could turn out to be far more advantageous than you might think. This has potential to be one of your better days as far as financial progress is concerned and you should also be able to avoid running into the buffers in personal matters. A good deal more optimism seems to be on offer.

14 FRIDAY
Moon Age Day 16   Moon Sign Scorpio

am . . . .

pm . . . .
A continuation of your optimistic frame of mind should help you to open
all sorts of doors, though of course this doesn't necessarily mean you will
walk into any of them. It's all a matter of self-belief, something that
Pisces doesn't have in heaps. A day to grit your teeth and take a few
chances – it could really pay off!

15 SATURDAY
Moon Age Day 17   Moon Sign Scorpio

am . . . .

pm . . . .
If you discover that most people want to be in your good books at
present, this can be of great assistance across the weekend. Social
encounters could turn out very pleasantly indeed, as can current issues
associated with love. Why not make the weekend your own by being
willing to take the lead?

16 SUNDAY
Moon Age Day 18   Moon Sign Sagittarius

am . . . .

pm . . . .
High spirits tend to prevail under present trends and you are able to get
away with just about anything. A little cheek goes a long way and you are
so charming to know that you can convince most of those you meet to
offer their help. Whether you could have got by without it is a different
matter altogether.

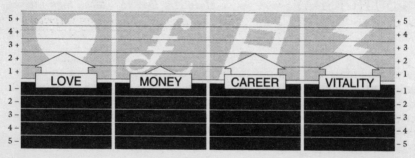

17 MONDAY   *Moon Age Day 19   Moon Sign Sagittarius*

am . . . .

pm . . . .
Even if career matters keep you very busy at the start of a new working
week, you also need to find time to look after the interests of those you
love. Your partner might be going through a few problems, whilst
you can offer younger family members especially a great deal of
your experience.

18 TUESDAY   *Moon Age Day 20   Moon Sign Sagittarius*

am . . . .

pm . . . .
If you decide to use today to improve your social life, you may not
have very much spare time. It is important not to carry the need to
please others to extremes. People like you the way you are and probably
won't be any fonder of you just because you are trying to do everything
for them.

19 WEDNESDAY   *Moon Age Day 21   Moon Sign Capricorn*

am . . . .

pm . . . .
This has potential to be a rather pleasant period, during which you are
able to bring out the best in almost everyone you meet. Intuition is as
strong as ever and you might find that you are exceptionally curious
about the way life works. A little investigation seems to be on the cards
and could yield some unusual results.

20 THURSDAY   *Moon Age Day 22   Moon Sign Capricorn*

am . . . .

pm . . . .
Mars has now moved into your solar fifth house, which is better for
domestic matters and also offers you a greater amount of energy for
creative pursuits. The only potentially unfortunate fact is that it might
enlarge your ego a bit too. Maybe that's not a bad thing at all for a zodiac
sign that is usually too modest.

21 FRIDAY
Moon Age Day 23   Moon Sign Aquarius

am . . . .

pm . . . : . . . .
It might be best to let the rest of the world go by for a day or two. With a twelfth-house Moon you tend to be very contemplative and not at all inclined to push yourself more than is necessary. This would be a good time to take a short trip, just as long as there were cultural and intellectual advantages to be had.

22 SATURDAY
Moon Age Day 24   Moon Sign Aquarius

am . . . .

pm . . . .
Romance looks good again, though you would be wise to approach it in a quiet way rather than ruffling any feathers by showing your affection for more than one person. You are able to stand and look at life as if it were a movie projected just for you, a fact that allows you a unique and useful perspective.

23 SUNDAY
Moon Age Day 25   Moon Sign Pisces

am . . . .

pm . . . .
Communication matters have an effervescent quality and you will be able to make a powerful impact on the world at large. The lunar high coincides with a Sunday, so although that might prevent you from using all that energy at work, you can make the most of it by doing as much as you can to enliven your social life.

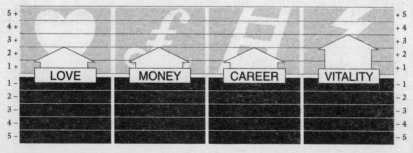

24 MONDAY
Moon Age Day 26   Moon Sign Pisces

am . . . .

pm . . . .
You can keep your spirits up today, and there is no better way to start a new week than with the Moon in your own zodiac sign. You needn't take no for an answer if you are certain of your position, and you can afford to take a few calculated risks in order to get exactly what you want from life.

25 TUESDAY
Moon Age Day 27   Moon Sign Aries

am . . . .

pm . . . .
You can continue to use good luck to help you towards your objectives, even though the Moon has now moved out of your zodiac sign. Those higher up the career tree can now be the source of significant support and should listen carefully to your ideas. What is even better is that your accustomed shyness seems to have taken a holiday.

26 WEDNESDAY
Moon Age Day 28   Moon Sign Aries

am . . . .

pm . . . .
A phase emphasising creative powers comes courtesy of the ever-strengthening position of Mars in your solar chart. There is virtually nothing that is beyond your present capabilities, just as long as you believe in yourself. On the way you might have to persuade someone else that you know what you are doing.

27 THURSDAY
Moon Age Day 0   Moon Sign Taurus

am . . . .

pm . . . .
You can elicit positive responses from most people today and that is partly because of your own present attitude to life. Meetings with strangers could turn out to be very surprising indeed and might offer you new incentives you hadn't even thought about. Stand by to make this one of the most eventful periods of the month.

28 FRIDAY
Moon Age Day 1   Moon Sign Taurus

am . . . .

pm . . . .
You can now use influences from relatively unexpected directions to help you along the path to success. Life can be quite strange at times for the average Piscean and today offers the chance to meet people who will have a profound bearing on your thoughts for the future. You ought to recognise them instinctively.

29 SATURDAY
Moon Age Day 2   Moon Sign Gemini

am . . . .

pm . . . .
This would be an ideal time during which to put new ideas to the test. Getting your own way in important negotiations should not be difficult, especially if they include other family members. The romantic side of Pisces is quite clearly on display and you are able to strengthen attachments all round.

30 SUNDAY
Moon Age Day 3   Moon Sign Gemini

am . . . .

pm . . . .
Your love life continues to be a source of potential joy and is made all the better by the arrival of a Sunday on which you shouldn't have to do too much in a concrete sense. You can recognise compromise in the attitude of your partner or sweetheart, and you know just the right words to make people melt.

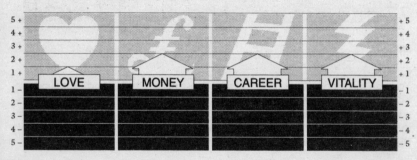

May 2006

YOUR MONTH AT A GLANCE

⊕ = Opportunities are around   ⊖ = Be on the defensive   ⬤ = Life is pretty ordinary

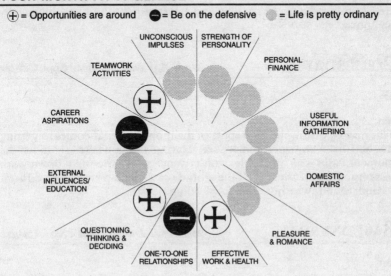

UNCONSCIOUS IMPULSES
STRENGTH OF PERSONALITY
PERSONAL FINANCE
TEAMWORK ACTIVITIES
CAREER ASPIRATIONS
USEFUL INFORMATION GATHERING
EXTERNAL INFLUENCES/ EDUCATION
DOMESTIC AFFAIRS
QUESTIONING, THINKING & DECIDING
ONE-TO-ONE RELATIONSHIPS
EFFECTIVE WORK & HEALTH
PLEASURE & ROMANCE

MAY HIGHS AND LOWS

Here I show you how the rhythms of the Moon will affect you this month. Like the tide, your energies and abilities will rise and fall with its pattern. When it is above the centre line, go for it, when it is below, you should be resting.

HIGH 21ST–22ND

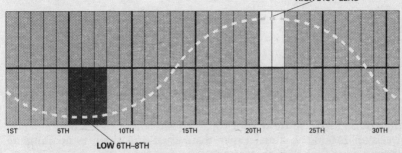

1ST   5TH   10TH   15TH   20TH   25TH   30TH

LOW 6TH–8TH

1 MONDAY

Moon Age Day 4   Moon Sign Gemini

am . . . .

pm . . . .
Whilst nostalgic matters could take on an agreeable aspect at the beginning of this month, you can also make the most of excitement in your home life. Career issues could be less fortunate, particularly if you are not using the necessary time and effort required to keep things fully on course.

2 TUESDAY

Moon Age Day 5   Moon Sign Cancer

am . . . .

pm . . . .
This may be one of the high spots of the month when it comes to getting the best from romance and leisure. Having fun is where it's at for the moment, and you probably won't want to be too tied down with responsibilities of any sort. If the attitude of a friend proves to be difficult to understand, why not ask a few leading questions?

3 WEDNESDAY

Moon Age Day 6   Moon Sign Cancer

am . . . .

pm . . . .
You should now be able to express yourself very clearly and you won't have the least difficulty in getting your message across the way you intend. The Sun is now in your solar third house, which has to be good for co-operative ventures of any sort and even if you are happy in a group, you tend to lead it much of the time.

4 THURSDAY

Moon Age Day 7   Moon Sign Leo

am . . . .

pm . . . .
A major boost to career prospects is now possible with a combination of solar and lunar positions in your solar chart. This is definitely the right time during May to show your capabilities to those who have influence. Decision making is much easier than usual and there is no jumping around from foot to foot, as is often the case for Pisces.

5 FRIDAY

Moon Age Day 8   Moon Sign Leo

am . . . .

pm . . . .
You would be wise to get tedious tasks out of the way early in the day, leaving yourself with the time to do what you want later. You should already be planning for what could be an excellent weekend but you will need to let others know your ideas early. By the evening you should be contemplating ways to please those you care for.

6 SATURDAY

Moon Age Day 9   Moon Sign Virgo

am . . . .

pm . . . .
This has potential to be one of your better days as far as finances are concerned, despite the lunar low, and you should be doing everything you can to please the people who occupy your thoughts. New activities could appeal, and there is a definite desire to get out and about. You may consider that you have been stuck indoors too much of late.

7 SUNDAY

Moon Age Day 10   Moon Sign Virgo

am . . . .

pm . . . .
Today's trends suggest that you may not be completely in charge of practical matters, and may decide to defer to the opinions of people who seem to know better. All the same, don't take anything for granted because things are not always what they seem. A good dose of intuition helps you to make the right choices.

8 MONDAY
Moon Age Day 11   Moon Sign Virgo

am ....

pm ....
This would not be the best day of the month to tempt fate. There could be unexpected changes coming about in your daily life and perhaps you would be best off leaving major decisions until tomorrow. Even if the lunar low restricts you this month, you needn't allow it to leave any real problems in its wake.

9 TUESDAY
Moon Age Day 12   Moon Sign Libra

am ....

pm ....
Your mental skills are well accented around this time and it shouldn't be at all difficult to work out how anyone is likely to react under given circumstances. A day to work according to your own mind and not to spend too much time thinking about what others would do. You are more than capable right now.

10 WEDNESDAY
Moon Age Day 13   Moon Sign Libra

am ....

pm ....
There might be challenges to your ability to keep life on an even keel right now, and that won't be too comfortable. You might get the impression that one or two of the people with whom you associate, especially at work, are simply playing silly games. That's fine, but you don't have to join in.

11 THURSDAY
Moon Age Day 14   Moon Sign Scorpio

am ....

pm ....
In terms of cash you can make the most of a period that is slightly luckier than of late. Venus is in your solar second house and will offer better fortune generally, though not perhaps in a particularly big way. There are advantages to putting yourself at the front of almost any queue at this stage of the week.

12 FRIDAY
Moon Age Day 15   Moon Sign Scorpio

am . . . .

pm . . . .
Intellectual matters can now prove to be most rewarding, offering you scope to be chasing new ideas for most of today. The things that are going on out there in the wider world should be of particular interest and there isn't much doubt about your ability to change successfully with different circumstances.

13 SATURDAY
Moon Age Day 16   Moon Sign Scorpio

am . . . .

pm . . . .
There could be the odd power struggle as far as your personal life is concerned, though not if you refuse to join in. The attitude of friends might also be somewhat strange at this time and you may not find it very easy to get people on side. This weekend demands just a little thought on your part.

14 SUNDAY
Moon Age Day 17   Moon Sign Sagittarius

am . . . .

pm . . . .
Influences could come along today that you can use to point you in the right direction when it comes to career and professional developments. That doesn't necessarily mean you are doing anything about them right now, particularly if you are mainly committed to more social aspects on this May Sunday.

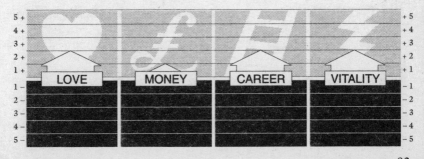

15 MONDAY   *Moon Age Day 18   Moon Sign Sagittarius*

am . . . .

pm . . . .
Why not find out what is going on in the world by asking a few sensible questions? There are gains to be made simply from being in the right place at the best time, and your intuition should tell you where and when to act. As far as your career is concerned, you are in a position to gain assistance from unusual directions.

16 TUESDAY   *Moon Age Day 19   Moon Sign Capricorn*

am . . . .

pm . . . .
Though you probably should avoid impulse buying for the moment, there are bargains to be had if you look around carefully. You could also be on the receiving end of unexpected gifts from friends or loved ones. Financial deals can be turned in your favour with just a little extra thought on your part.

17 WEDNESDAY   *Moon Age Day 20   Moon Sign Capricorn*

am . . . .

pm . . . .
New encounters could prove to be quite inspiring around now and you need to turn your mind outward, rather than sitting and thinking about things in your own little corner. Even if you are inclined to be quite introspective at the moment, you will probably only find the answers you seek out in the wider world.

18 THURSDAY   *Moon Age Day 21   Moon Sign Capricorn*

am . . . .

pm . . . .
Beware of believing everything you hear today because not everyone will prove to be equally reliable. There are misleading influences around and it is possible you could spend quite some time walking down a path that leads to nothing but a dead end. Once again you need to call your intuition into play.

19 FRIDAY
Moon Age Day 22   Moon Sign Aquarius

am . . . .

pm . . . .
Trends encourage a very strong urge for freedom within your mind.
Actually doing exactly what you want may not be too easy, because the
Moon is in your solar twelfth house. Minor frustrations could be the
result, because at the same time the planet Mars has the power to urge
you on.

20 SATURDAY
Moon Age Day 23   Moon Sign Aquarius

am . . . .

pm . . . .
There are new initiatives on offer. Even if you can see them and know
exactly how you ought to react, until the lunar high comes along
tomorrow you would be better off planning, rather than actually doing
anything concrete. People you don't see too often may be making a
return visit to your life during the weekend.

21 SUNDAY
Moon Age Day 24   Moon Sign Pisces

am . . . .

pm . . . .
You have what it takes to make the most of social and personal
advantages around now, and the lunar high assists you in almost every
sphere of your life. Although it might be difficult to push ahead
professionally on a Sunday, you can use today's influences to make the
best possible impression on the world.

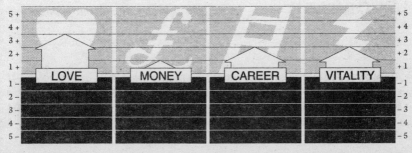

22 MONDAY
Moon Age Day 25   Moon Sign Pisces

am . . . .

pm . . . .

Progress has potential to be generally good and you have a strong pioneering spirit at the beginning of this week that is sure to help you on your way. You can get Lady Luck on your side, and although taking chances is not something you do very often, you can afford to be chancing your arm now.

23 TUESDAY
Moon Age Day 26   Moon Sign Aries

am . . . .

pm . . . .

Domestic matters could prove highly satisfying today, even if you are not making quite the practical progress you had hoped for. Romance is also on the cards and you are able to make a good impression on someone coming new into your life. Established relationships can now be given some sort of boost.

24 WEDNESDAY
Moon Age Day 27   Moon Sign Aries

am . . . .

pm . . . .

Trends now encourage you to acquire any particular items you've had in mind, be they for business or pleasure. Maybe you have been waiting for something to arrive in the post or else there has been a delay or some sort. For whatever reason, this might end up feeling slightly like your birthday.

25 THURSDAY
Moon Age Day 28   Moon Sign Taurus

am . . . .

pm . . . .

A positive element is evident today, no matter what you decide to do. It could be that you can persuade people who have proved to be somewhat awkward in the recent past to take a more considered attitude. On the other hand, it is possible that your persuasive powers prove to be extremely useful with family members.

26 FRIDAY   *Moon Age Day 29   Moon Sign Taurus*

am . . . .

pm . . . .
You can capitalise on a new positive phase as far as domestic matters generally are concerned, thanks to the position of Mercury in your solar fourth house. Shared ideals and interests should be quite fulfilling and you are able to reach a consensus with your partner that doesn't seem to have been present of late.

27 SATURDAY   *Moon Age Day 0   Moon Sign Gemini*

am . . . .

pm . . . .
In a domestic sense it appears that situations are still looking good, though if life lacks a certain degree of sparkle you may decide to move your mind and body out of the house. Excitement is possible,but you may have to work a little to find it. Why not enlist the support of friends who think in a similar way to you?

28 SUNDAY   *Moon Age Day 1   Moon Sign Gemini*

am . . . .

pm . . . .
Hasty purchases and expensive investments are definitely to be avoided right now. Your best approach is to settle for the simple things in life and not to push for items you don't really need and probably do not even want. Buyer's remorse could well be the result if you spend money unnecessarily this Sunday.

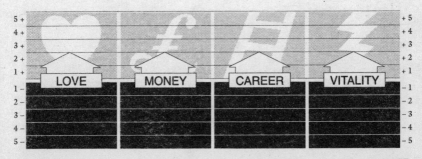

29 MONDAY

Moon Age Day 2   Moon Sign Cancer

am . . . .

pm . . . .
A far more personally enlivening period is now on offer. You have a chance to show the world just who you are. Meanwhile personal creativity could well be going off the scale. Romance and leisure activities receive a definite boost at the start of a week that ought to suit you in many different ways.

30 TUESDAY

Moon Age Day 3   Moon Sign Cancer

am . . . .

pm . . . .
Venus is now in your solar third house. This is a light-hearted influence that has potential to bring out the best in you. It shouldn't be difficult for you to persuade others to join in your present happy frame of mind and to make sure there are plenty of laughs as a result. There will be a few miseries about too – but that's life.

31 WEDNESDAY

Moon Age Day 4   Moon Sign Leo

am . . . .

pm . . . .
A strongly supportive influence from more than one quarter is what you can make use of today. The planets are still looking particularly strong for you and the Sun occupies your solar fourth house. A certain concern for those to whom you are related is possible for the next couple of weeks, though probably not necessary.

1 THURSDAY

Moon Age Day 5   Moon Sign Leo

am . . . .

pm . . . .
Even if you are now quite ready to put yourself under the spotlight, your present forthright approach to life might prove to be too much for one or two individuals. You might need to modify your stance, according to the person you are dealing with. This is not a difficult process for the Piscean, even if it can prove somewhat confusing.

2 FRIDAY

Moon Age Day 6   Moon Sign Leo

am . . . .

pm . . . .
Trends assist you to be happiest when you are out there in the social mainstream. The weekend might start early for some Pisces subjects, particularly if you deliberately choose to spend more time doing what pleases you. Avoid getting involved in discussions that could easily turn into totally pointless arguments.

3 SATURDAY

Moon Age Day 7   Moon Sign Virgo

am . . . .

pm . . . .
Keeping a fairly low profile is quite sensible for today. The lunar low could take away some of the driving force that has been present in your nature. This needn't be a miserable day, but it could make greater demands on you. It might be better to let other people take some of the strain with domestic chores.
s

4 SUNDAY

Moon Age Day 8   Moon Sign Virgo

am . . . .

pm . . . .
Forget the feeling that the grass looks greener on the other side of the fence. It isn't. There may be some fairly unstable situations around as far as your life generally is concerned and you need to be quite circumspect. Don't be too quick to jump to conclusions about your love life.

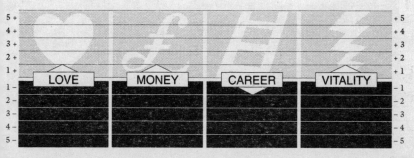

June 2006

YOUR MONTH AT A GLANCE

⊕ = Opportunities are around   ⊖ = Be on the defensive   ⬤ = Life is pretty ordinary

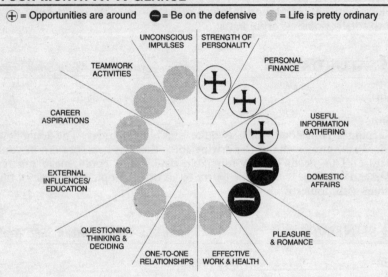

UNCONSCIOUS IMPULSES
STRENGTH OF PERSONALITY
PERSONAL FINANCE
TEAMWORK ACTIVITIES
CAREER ASPIRATIONS
USEFUL INFORMATION GATHERING
EXTERNAL INFLUENCES/ EDUCATION
DOMESTIC AFFAIRS
QUESTIONING, THINKING & DECIDING
PLEASURE & ROMANCE
ONE-TO-ONE RELATIONSHIPS
EFFECTIVE WORK & HEALTH

JUNE HIGHS AND LOWS

Here I show you how the rhythms of the Moon will affect you this month. Like the tide, your energies and abilities will rise and fall with its pattern. When it is above the centre line, go for it, when it is below, you should be resting.

HIGH 17TH–18TH

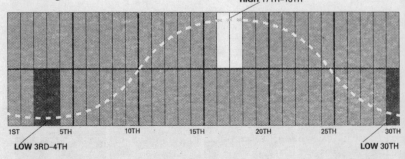

1ST   5TH   10TH   15TH   20TH   25TH   30TH

LOW 3RD–4TH

LOW 30TH

90

5 MONDAY
Moon Age Day 9   Moon Sign Libra

am ....

pm ....
The current state of relationships in your life could well put a definite smile on your face. The Sun remains in your solar fourth house, which is good for all family matters, and you should find that you can reach a consensus with anyone who has been quite awkward of late. The time is right to launch some new ideas.

6 TUESDAY
Moon Age Day 10   Moon Sign Libra

am ....

pm ....
Places of leisure and entertainment could hold a special appeal for you around now. There may well be some surprises on offer, and a few of them are especially heart-warming. If friends have specific needs of you under present planetary trends, as usual you should be pleased to help them out.

7 WEDNESDAY
Moon Age Day 11   Moon Sign Libra

am ....

pm ....
You would wise to avoid minor conflicts with co-workers. These are not only unnecessary but get in the way of the sort of progress you should be making. Not everyone may be on the same wavelength as you at the moment, no matter how hard you try to make it so. Some small financial gains could be possible later in the day.

8 THURSDAY
Moon Age Day 12   Moon Sign Scorpio

am ....

pm ....
Present trends encourage a desire to live for the moment. This way of thinking can have some beneficial effects. For example, when it comes to journeys planned at the last moment you are likely to be right in your element. Meanwhile, you can attract help from people further up the career tree than you are.

9 FRIDAY
Moon Age Day 13   Moon Sign Scorpio

am . . . .

pm . . . .
Your home life could bring a tendency towards laziness and for once you may be happy to let others take some of the strain. It is important all the same to keep track of everything that is happening around you because there is a good chance of making some last-minute decisions that will benefit you significantly.

10 SATURDAY
Moon Age Day 14   Moon Sign Sagittarius

am . . . .

pm . . . .
This has potential to be a smooth period when it comes to professional progress, though of course the trend is a little wasted if you don't work at the weekend. Forward planning is also possible right now, though you can also afford to spend some time doing whatever takes your fancy, in the company of people who make you laugh.

11 SUNDAY
Moon Age Day 15   Moon Sign Sagittarius

am . . . .

pm . . . .
Romantic involvements are positively highlighted on this June Sunday. Spend some time with the person who means the most to you and you won't regret it. A day to seek out intelligent conversation and avoid noisy or irksome people. You might decide the time is right to take a short journey to somewhere particularly interesting.

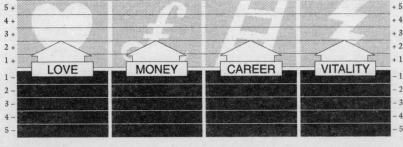

12 MONDAY
Moon Age Day 16   Moon Sign Capricorn

am . . . .

pm . . . .
Today you have scope to enjoy the lighter side of life and may not be taking anything very seriously. You are a natural joker at the moment and can bring significant pleasure into the lives of other people on the way. Confidence remains generally high, perhaps inclining you to be more talkative than usual.

13 TUESDAY
Moon Age Day 17   Moon Sign Capricorn

am . . . .

pm . . . .
The Sun remains in your solar fourth house, making this an ideal time to get on well with people who are familiar to you. The distant past seems to offer a few rewards under present trends and you have everything necessary to make this an eventful and quite useful sort of day as long as you don't get too nostalgic.

14 WEDNESDAY
Moon Age Day 18   Moon Sign Capricorn

am . . . .

pm . . . .
There might be a slightly edgy atmosphere at work, something you would be wise to work against throughout most of today. It is not likely to be you who is causing the problems and they probably won't have much of a bearing on your life if you choose to spend at least some time on your own.

15 THURSDAY
Moon Age Day 19   Moon Sign Aquarius

am . . . .

pm . . . .
Mercury's position in your solar chart allows you to stand out more. This could mean you are being watched, something that might not be entirely comfortable all the time. The more extroverted side of your nature is beginning to show though, and you shouldn't worry too much if people are singling you out.

16 FRIDAY
Moon Age Day 20   Moon Sign Aquarius

am . . . .

pm . . . .
You may now decide to get involved in deeper, emotional matters, and you should also be making the most of domestic concerns and nostalgic situations. The Moon is in your solar twelfth house so there is likely to be quite a wistful side to your nature, though you can change this situation quickly by tomorrow.

17 SATURDAY
Moon Age Day 21   Moon Sign Pisces

am . . . .

pm . . . .
Stand by for the lunar high, which could manifest itself in a number of different ways this month. Any competition can be outdone as you stride easily towards your chosen objectives. An important deal could be clinched under these trends and you are about as dynamic and certain as Pisces can be!

18 SUNDAY
Moon Age Day 22   Moon Sign Pisces

am . . . .

pm . . . .
Mental and physical strength could now be at a peak and this is the part of the month during which you can afford to take your life fully into your own hands. You probably won't mind taking the odd chance and may even be leading the field in some way. In terms of conversation, you can talk to anyone at the moment.

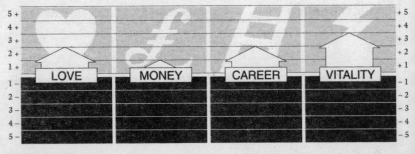

19 MONDAY
Moon Age Day 23   Moon Sign Aries

am . . . .

pm . . . .
Trends now indicate that places of entertainment are a must at the start
of this week. It isn't out of the question that you have chosen this time
to take a break, in which case you can travel wherever takes your fancy.
Even if you are stuck with the usual routines, you can find ways to alter
them and to make life more interesting.

20 TUESDAY
Moon Age Day 24   Moon Sign Aries

am . . . .

pm . . . .
In a domestic sense you have scope to fill your life with contentment,
though the Sun will soon change its position in your chart so you need
to make the most of the homely trends. Professionally speaking, life
might seem less interesting, which is why you need to use this time to
please yourself in other ways.

21 WEDNESDAY
Moon Age Day 25   Moon Sign Taurus

am . . . .

pm . . . .
You have what it takes to move mountains, though only at your own
speed. Don't be rushed at present, and be willing to take your time in
getting where you want to be. Pisces needs extra stimulus now,
particularly in a romantic sense, and you may decide to ring the changes
with regard to friendship.

22 THURSDAY
Moon Age Day 26   Moon Sign Taurus

am . . . .

pm . . . .
Material and practical issues should prove to be the number one in your
life now that Mars occupies your solar sixth house. If you are a little
touchy at times, people will forgive you, but the real problem comes in
forgiving yourself. Pisces can be the most pleasant of all the zodiac signs,
but remorse is its middle name.

23 FRIDAY
Moon Age Day 27   Moon Sign Gemini

am . . . .

pm . . . .
Attention is now focused on your own ego, which is potentially stronger than it has been for quite some time. You can derive great pleasure from entertaining others, and shouldn't be in the least concerned if the spotlight is upon you. Pisces needs to shine sometimes and it looks as though this is such a period.

24 SATURDAY
Moon Age Day 28   Moon Sign Gemini

am . . . .

pm . . . .
You really should be able to enjoy home comforts this weekend and can make great gains just from being amongst the people you care for the most. If you decide to take a trip of any sort, it is most likely to be in the company of family members, and the regard you have for younger people is enhanced under present trends.

25 SUNDAY
Moon Age Day 29   Moon Sign Cancer

am . . . .

pm . . . .
You have scope to make the most of whatever is happening in love relationships at present. Romantic encounters could come thick and fast for those Pisceans who have been looking for love, whilst if you are in a settled attachment, you will find ways to pep it up and to bring more excitement to bear.

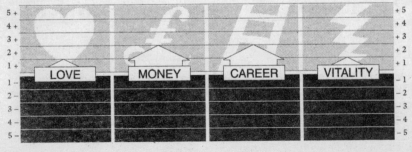

26 MONDAY
Moon Age Day 0   Moon Sign Cancer

am . . . .

pm . . . .
You have potential to keep up quite an impressive front socially, even if that means that some of the responsibilities of life are slightly shelved for the moment. There could be an easing of tension with regard to a long-standing row, though of course this may not be anything for which you are personally responsible.

27 TUESDAY
Moon Age Day 1   Moon Sign Cancer

am . . . .

pm . . . .
Trends indicate that you might have to struggle somewhat today to keep work matters on track and that you would do well to accept the proffered advice and help of colleagues. If you insist on going it alone, you will work twice as hard and might still not achieve your objectives. Too much pride is definitely not a good thing at the moment.

28 WEDNESDAY
Moon Age Day 2   Moon Sign Leo

am . . . .

pm . . . .
Right now practical aims and objectives should prove much easier and you may even decide that you don't want to be bothered with details. As a direct contrast to yesterday you can afford to be relaxed and easy-going. The attitude of a friend might prove to be rather surprising at some stage.

29 THURSDAY
Moon Age Day 3   Moon Sign Leo

am . . . .

pm . . . .
Being in the know professionally can make all the difference to you today, and it's important to keep asking the right questions. The attitude of family members might be difficult to understand but once again you need to ask the right questions. With plenty to play for in the financial stakes, you can make efforts to become better off.

30 FRIDAY
Moon Age Day 4   Moon Sign Virgo

am ....

pm ....
Vitality could well be in fairly short supply, so you would be wise to keep your expectations rather modest. The lunar low has potential to sap some of your strength and at the same time you could find that you are subject to the will of those around you. Not a good day for gambling or taking risks of any sort.

1 SATURDAY
Moon Age Day 5   Moon Sign Virgo

am ....

pm ....
If morale is somewhat low at present, your best response is to turn down heavy responsibilities and leave room for possible errors. You might decide to stay close to home today and may not be too keen to push the bounds of the credible. This is a very good day for thinking ahead and for planning instead of doing too much.

2 SUNDAY
Moon Age Day 6   Moon Sign Virgo

am ....

pm ....
Things won't necessarily go according to plan, but you can improve your situation as the day goes on. If you need to recharge your batteries, you can do so wonderfully by just being in the company of people you hold dear. An atmospheric time with regard to romance could be on offer by the evening.

July 2006

YOUR MONTH AT A GLANCE

⊕ = Opportunities are around   ⊖ = Be on the defensive   ◐ = Life is pretty ordinary

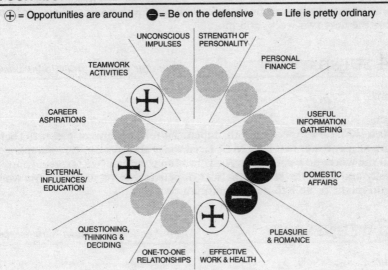

- UNCONSCIOUS IMPULSES
- STRENGTH OF PERSONALITY
- PERSONAL FINANCE
- TEAMWORK ACTIVITIES
- CAREER ASPIRATIONS
- USEFUL INFORMATION GATHERING
- EXTERNAL INFLUENCES/ EDUCATION
- DOMESTIC AFFAIRS
- QUESTIONING, THINKING & DECIDING
- PLEASURE & ROMANCE
- ONE-TO-ONE RELATIONSHIPS
- EFFECTIVE WORK & HEALTH

JULY HIGHS AND LOWS

Here I show you how the rhythms of the Moon will affect you this month. Like the tide, your energies and abilities will rise and fall with its pattern. When it is above the centre line, go for it, when it is below, you should be resting.

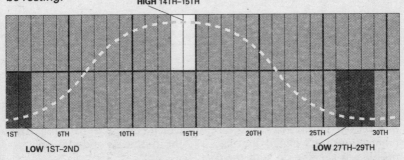

HIGH 14TH–15TH

1ST   5TH   10TH   15TH   20TH   25TH   30TH

LOW 1ST–2ND

LOW 27TH–29TH

3 MONDAY
Moon Age Day 7   Moon Sign Libra

am . . . .

pm . . . .
Love and romance are likely to be foremost in your mind at present and
they continue to be so for a few days to come. It pays to extend your
social life too by going out and finding new contacts. Freedom is
important whilst the Sun occupies your solar fifth house, where it will be
for the next two weeks and more.

4 TUESDAY
Moon Age Day 8   Moon Sign Libra

am . . . .

pm . . . .
You shouldn't expect smooth, superficial relationships at present. There
are deeper issues that have to be faced today and that can throw a spanner
in the works now and again. A day to keep your patience, express yourself
fully and leave the rest to the sort of person you naturally are. At work
you might be able to make significant progress.

5 WEDNESDAY   ☿
Moon Age Day 9   Moon Sign Scorpio

am . . . .

pm . . . .
Life offers excitement for many Piscean subjects now. There could well
be sudden changes of direction and a desire to do things simply for the
thrill. Trends encourage your spirit to be unfettered at the moment and
when Pisces is in this frame of mind, anything at all is possible. You can
persuade friends to be especially co-operative.

6 THURSDAY   ☿
Moon Age Day 10   Moon Sign Scorpio

am . . . .

pm . . . .
The signs are that an issue related to your private life could be fulfilling
and enjoyable. You may be able to put yourself in the company of a friend
or a relative you haven't seen recently, which could also have important
implications. It's all go for Pisces at the moment, and the only real
problem is keeping up with the pace.

7 FRIDAY ☿ *Moon Age Day 11   Moon Sign Scorpio*

am . . . .

pm . . . .
Romance can seem larger than life itself. Pisceans may well be in an over-nostalgic mood for today, and that can bring its own little problems. You need to retain a degree of realism but the present position of the Moon might make that rather difficult. In a more practical sense there could be new options on offer at work.

8 SATURDAY ☿ *Moon Age Day 12   Moon Sign Sagittarius*

am . . . .

pm . . . .
Professionally speaking this could be the time to bring something to a satisfactory conclusion – that is if you work at the weekend. Otherwise, what you might have on your mind is fun, and you won't want to be diverted from a particular plan you just know is going to suit everyone. Maybe you should think again.

9 SUNDAY ☿ *Moon Age Day 13   Moon Sign Sagittarius*

am . . . .

pm . . . .
Bigger and better things can be made to happen now. Mars has moved in your solar chart and its influence stirs things up no end. Avoid conflict, especially if the people with whom you can't see eye-to-eye are so obviously wrong. There probably won't be too much time for pointless details at present.

10 MONDAY ☿ *Moon Age Day 14   Moon Sign Capricorn*

am . . . .

pm . . . .
Today could turn out to be quite an exceptional period and one during which your best option is to get away from your usual routines in order to meet new people. The greater the stimulus that you can bring into your life at the moment, the better you will respond. Ordinary situations could seem quite boring!

11 TUESDAY ☿ *Moon Age Day 15   Moon Sign Capricorn*

am . . . .

pm . . . .
As your seek to express your identity more and more, so it might seem that other people are trying in some way to hold you back. Even if they are doing nothing of the sort, they could be trying to warn you against making mistakes. In the end the choice is yours, but you do need to sit and think things through carefully.

12 WEDNESDAY ☿ *Moon Age Day 16   Moon Sign Aquarius*

am . . . .

pm . . . .
You can afford to trust your intuition right now and there could be good insights into the personal dilemmas your friends are going through. Handing out advice is easy for Pisces at the best of times, but especially so under present trends. Why not save time later in the day to do something that really takes your fancy?

13 THURSDAY ☿ *Moon Age Day 17   Moon Sign Aquarius*

am . . . .

pm . . . .
A more exuberant time at work is now possible, though you may lack a little earthy realism that could help you more than your present dreams. You would be wise to listen carefully to what someone with either greater age or experience is saying, especially if they appear to know something important that you don't.

14 FRIDAY ☿ *Moon Age Day 18   Moon Sign Pisces*

am . . . .

pm . . . .
Along comes the lunar high, and together with existing planetary trends it enables you to increase your persuasive powers no end. Personal partnerships can be improved too and it seems as though you have the magic formula when it comes to getting on with just about anyone you come across today.

15 SATURDAY ☿ *Moon Age Day 19   Moon Sign Pisces*

am . . . .

pm . . . .
Stand by for a phase during which you can make good use of a great deal of charisma and personal attractiveness. There could be new opportunities for romance, and the lunar high continues to support you in your efforts to get ahead generally. With everything to play for, this is the time to let your light shine.

16 SUNDAY ☿ *Moon Age Day 20   Moon Sign Aries*

am . . . .

pm . . . .
Mars brings you the ability to get down to the root issues of any professional matter. You are unlikely to allow anything to stand in your way and woe betide anyone who tries to cross you at the moment. Comfort and security may be far from your mind under present trends and you can afford to go for gold, no matter what.

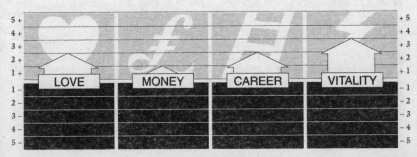

17 MONDAY ☿ *Moon Age Day 21 Moon Sign Aries*

am . . . .

pm . . . .
The time is right to back your hunches when it comes to financial transactions, and not to be put off by setbacks. There could be some good luck around later in the day and it might be a mistake to sort out too much early on. Confidence to do the right thing is still present, though one or two people could prove awkward at the moment.

18 TUESDAY ☿ *Moon Age Day 22 Moon Sign Taurus*

am . . . .

pm . . . .
The main emphasis is on communication and trends encourage a strong desire to improve your social life in a number of different ways. The quiet aspect of Pisces appears to be taking a holiday because you are so keen to make everyone and his dog listen to what you have to say.

19 WEDNESDAY ☿ *Moon Age Day 23 Moon Sign Taurus*

am . . . .

pm . . . .
The potential for new love interest is formidable. This is a period during which you can make good use of your powers of attraction and a magnetism that others find difficult to avoid. The only slightly negative side of this is that you might be attracting the wrong sort of attention – which could lead to a little embarrassment all round.

20 THURSDAY ☿ *Moon Age Day 24 Moon Sign Taurus*

am . . . .

pm . . . .
This has potential to be a quieter and less demanding sort of day, which is probably no bad thing after such a hectic period. If home life and general domesticity appeal to you, you may well decide to spend every moment you can in the company of those you care about the most. Younger people can offer their own special joy.

21 FRIDAY ☿ *Moon Age Day 25* *Moon Sign Gemini*

am . . . .

pm . . . .
Getting an early start on work projects would be no bad thing. Any excess of energy can be used to ensure that much can be accomplished, though nobody ought to get in the way of progress and you need to keep your eye on your ultimate objectives. Life can be like an emotional seesaw at present and getting enough breaks could be difficult.

22 SATURDAY ☿ *Moon Age Day 26* *Moon Sign Gemini*

am . . . .

pm . . . .
Venus is now in your solar fifth house, bringing stronger indications of something new happening, either romantically or socially. Either way, you can make this a particularly interesting sort of weekend, and can take advantage of new opportunities. You are still burning up masses of nervous energy so use it positively.

23 SUNDAY ☿ *Moon Age Day 27* *Moon Sign Cancer*

am . . . .

pm . . . .
You would be wise to impose some order on your working life, particularly if many details right now seem nebulous and even impossible. Self-discipline seems to be the way forward. Concentrate on one thing at once and don't be inclined to dissipate your energies by having to go back and put right mistakes all the time.

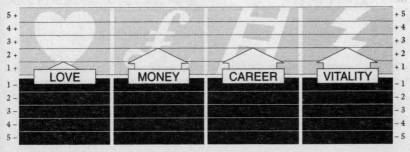

24 MONDAY ☿ *Moon Age Day 28   Moon Sign Cancer*

am . . . .

pm . . . .
You may decide you want to please yourself at the moment, and that can
be something of a problem at a time when the rest of the world seems to
be demanding your attention. Maybe you need to split the day carefully
– into those periods during which you are available, and others where you
get the chance to do what suits you.

25 TUESDAY ☿ *Moon Age Day 0   Moon Sign Leo*

am . . . .

pm . . . .
Trends suggest an expansive element at work, and you are able to co-
operate fully with colleagues. Pisces subjects who are between jobs at the
moment should concentrate a good deal of their energy into looking
around because there may well be options on offer. This would not be
the best day to gamble with finances.

26 WEDNESDAY ☿ *Moon Age Day 1   Moon Sign Leo*

am . . . .

pm . . . .
Even if there is much excitability to be found in your life around this
time, the challenge now comes in dealing with personal relationships.
You may be confronted by people who seem determined to be awkward,
or who fail to see what you consider to be a really sensible point of view.

27 THURSDAY ☿ *Moon Age Day 2   Moon Sign Virgo*

am . . . .

pm . . . .
As the lunar low arrives, you might be frustrated by the lack of potential
assistance you can attract from other people. If patience is running low,
you need to try and keep life as simple as possible. Routines might seem
tedious and yet you don't seem to have the incentive to break out of
them. Try to stay calm if you can.

28 FRIDAY ☿ *Moon Age Day 3   Moon Sign Virgo*

am . . . .

pm . . . .
Energy could still be lacking, but if that worries you, bear in mind that the lunar low only lasts for a couple of days, and rather than being concerned that you don't seem to be getting ahead, think in terms of forward planning. Knocking your head against a brick wall isn't likely to help at all under present trends.

29 SATURDAY ☿ *Moon Age Day 4   Moon Sign Virgo*

am . . . .

pm . . . .
There could be a few personal disappointments to be faced today, though in the fullness of time these won't seem so bad, and it's simply a case of realising that you are looking on the black side. Let situations take their own course and allow others to make the running, at least for now.

30 SUNDAY *Moon Age Day 5   Moon Sign Libra*

am . . . .

pm . . . .
You shouldn't take anything for granted now at a personal level. You may not be everyone's cup of tea today, but you need to be realistic and to avoid reactions that are out of proportion with reality. Even if spending a little time on your own seems attractive today, you might be better off finding some enjoyment with friends.

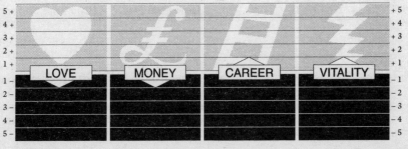

31 MONDAY
Moon Age Day 6   Moon Sign Libra

am . . . .

pm . . . .
Venus remains in your solar fifth house and is one of the major influences when it comes to attracting newcomers into your life. This is particularly true for Pisces people who are looking for romance that might lead to something long term. Friends generally could seem to be more approachable than they have been recently.

1 TUESDAY
Moon Age Day 7   Moon Sign Scorpio

am . . . .

pm . . . .
Recent efforts should now begin to show positive results. You can gain more control over your working environment and can attract assistance from unexpected directions. You can enlist valuable support from a number of different people and should be quite keen to put in that extra effort that will make all the difference.

2 WEDNESDAY
Moon Age Day 8   Moon Sign Scorpio

am . . . .

pm . . . .
A day to open yourself up to the unusual. This should assist you to move into the social spotlight as you continue to broaden your horizons. From an emotional point of view you are now less vulnerable that might sometimes be the case, and can talk openly about the way your mind is presently working.

3 THURSDAY
Moon Age Day 9   Moon Sign Scorpio

am . . . .

pm . . . .
If you allow yourself to be too assertive today, a friendship or even a deeper sort of relationships can offer problems further down the line. As a rule you are diplomatic and charming, qualities that you really do need to display at the moment. Conforming can be difficult, but is quite important under present trends.

4 FRIDAY
Moon Age Day 10   Moon Sign Sagittarius

am . . . .

pm . . . .
Now you can improve your lot by being in touch with people who inspire you. There are many possibilities that present themselves right now and in terms of your professional life you should be showing a greater amount of initiative. Hunches are worth following, because you have the ability to follow them through.

5 SATURDAY
Moon Age Day 11   Moon Sign Sagittarius

am . . . .

pm . . . .
Every effort should be made to leave doors open, especially when it comes to new relationships that are just developing. Even if you are still in the right frame of mind to take the initiative, in all probability this won't be necessary right now. In many spheres of your life the first and most simple observation will be the best one.

6 SUNDAY
Moon Age Day 12   Moon Sign Capricorn

am . . . .

pm . . . .
Looking after your own life is now a must and you probably won't take kindly to others interfering in your daily routines. In reality you might be best off relaxing a little. After all, the summer is really here now and you could gain a great deal by getting out into the fresh air with your partner or like-minded friends.

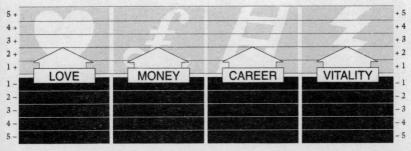

August 2006

YOUR MONTH AT A GLANCE

⊕ = Opportunities are around   ⊖ = Be on the defensive   ◯ = Life is pretty ordinary

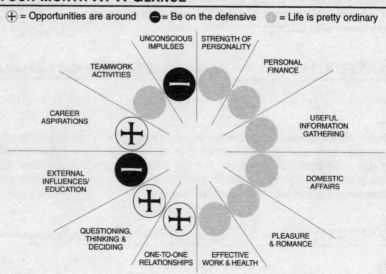

- UNCONSCIOUS IMPULSES
- STRENGTH OF PERSONALITY
- TEAMWORK ACTIVITIES
- PERSONAL FINANCE
- CAREER ASPIRATIONS
- USEFUL INFORMATION GATHERING
- EXTERNAL INFLUENCES/ EDUCATION
- DOMESTIC AFFAIRS
- QUESTIONING, THINKING & DECIDING
- ONE-TO-ONE RELATIONSHIPS
- EFFECTIVE WORK & HEALTH
- PLEASURE & ROMANCE

AUGUST HIGHS AND LOWS

Here I show you how the rhythms of the Moon will affect you this month. Like the tide, your energies and abilities will rise and fall with its pattern. When it is above the centre line, go for it, when it is below, you should be resting.

HIGH 11TH–12TH

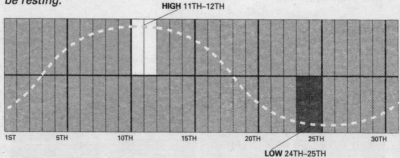

1ST   5TH   10TH   15TH   20TH   25TH   30TH

LOW 24TH–25TH

110

7 MONDAY *Moon Age Day 13   Moon Sign Capricorn*

am . . . .

pm . . . .
Benefits and support come from teamwork issues, and friends may help
to put your personal life into a better context. This is definitely a day on
which you should co-operate and during which you can get a great deal
done. There are signs that you may be coming near to the end of a
specific task that has been on your mind.

8 TUESDAY *Moon Age Day 14   Moon Sign Aquarius*

am . . . .

pm . . . .
You can expect the unexpected as far as your love life is concerned around
this time. You may not seem to be getting your own way, but in the end
you can bring people round to your specific point of view. Entertaining
might be fun, and you have scope to do your best to enjoy what the
summer has to offer.

9 WEDNESDAY *Moon Age Day 15   Moon Sign Aquarius*

am . . . .

pm . . . .
You may now run into some unavoidable setbacks and could be quieter
than you have been recently. The Moon in your solar twelfth house is the
culprit, but any difficulties shouldn't last long. The attitude of friends
might be somewhat awkward to accommodate with the way your own
mind is working around now.

10 THURSDAY *Moon Age Day 16   Moon Sign Aquarius*

am . . . .

pm . . . .
Before today is out you can take advantage of a general upward trend in
your life, but this may not make itself felt until the evening. In the
meantime trends encourage you to remain circumspect and not to push
your ideas forward, even if you are sure in your own mind that you know
what you are doing.

11 FRIDAY
Moon Age Day 17   Moon Sign Pisces

am . . . .

pm . . . .

By pulling strings at work it should now be possible to progress quickly and to get what you want from life in most ways. The lunar high gives you the ability to chance your arm, with every likelihood of success. You can persuade people to listen to what you are saying and trust your judgement automatically.

12 SATURDAY
Moon Age Day 18   Moon Sign Pisces

am . . . .

pm . . . .

There is an enhancement to relationships brought about by the present position of the Moon. This is the time to tell others exactly how you feel about them and a period during which you can afford to be firing on all cylinders. Don't wait to be asked, because you have to take the initiative as much as possible now.

13 SUNDAY
Moon Age Day 19   Moon Sign Aries

am . . . .

pm . . . .

There is a strong focus on luxury and the good things in life coming along for this Sunday. Getting out with friends or relatives would be no bad thing, because you perform better in groups as far as social trends are concerned. You tend to act very much on impulse right now but that can work well in the short term.

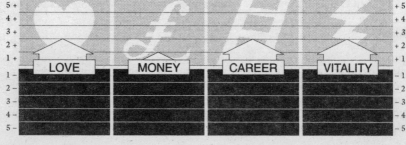

14 MONDAY
Moon Age Day 20   Moon Sign Aries

am . . . .

pm . . . .
This is a time of physical efficiency during which you can afford to burn up masses of energy and do yourself some good on the way. Others might find it difficult to maintain the sort of pace you are setting and could be surprised by your attitudes and actions around now.

15 TUESDAY
Moon Age Day 21   Moon Sign Taurus

am . . . .

pm . . . .
You can capitalise on strong support when you make choices today, especially at work. You can convince colleagues to fall in line with your opinions, and it is clear that your mind is focused. When you are not at work, intellectual pursuits of one sort or another are most likely to appeal to you.

16 WEDNESDAY
Moon Age Day 22   Moon Sign Taurus

am . . . .

pm . . . .
You should now be able to get many of your goals on target and can achieve beneficial results from most of your present efforts. Don't be sold short by anyone who has a vested interest in putting you down. Now is the time to stick up for what you believe to be true, even in the face of criticism.

17 THURSDAY
Moon Age Day 23   Moon Sign Gemini

am . . . .

pm . . . .
Even if intimate relationships now seem settled and cheerful, there could be one or two slight difficulties with family members or friends. The problem could be that you find it temporarily difficult to get on side with those who seem determined to throw a spanner in the works. Your usual patience is the key.

18 FRIDAY
Moon Age Day 24   Moon Sign Gemini

am . . . .

pm . . . .
A calmer time on the domestic scene is now possible, and probably a better understanding with friends. You may well decide to do something simple at home, particularly if you aren't anxious to get ahead at the moment. Some Pisces individuals could already be planning for the weekend.

19 SATURDAY
Moon Age Day 25   Moon Sign Cancer

am . . . .

pm . . . .
Payback can arise through taking the initiative in matters of the heart and you might also achieve an objective that might have looked a long way off. Beware of getting tied down with petty rules and regulations this weekend. Your best approach is to find a clear horizon during which you can do more or less whatever pleases you.

20 SUNDAY
Moon Age Day 26   Moon Sign Cancer

am . . . .

pm . . . .
It looks as though there is plenty to be done in a practical sense, and finding the space necessary to do what you want might be difficult. You tend to go from one job to the next though you can make these enjoyable if you plan ahead a little. Friends might be happy to join in, turning chores into pleasure.

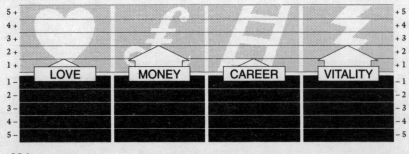

21 MONDAY
Moon Age Day 27   Moon Sign Leo

am ....

pm ....
Mercury is now in your solar sixth house and this offers a period during which you can sustain and enhance all practical matters. You are certainly on the ball as far as work is concerned and if you have been looking for advancement, your time may well be coming. Why not listen to the considered opinion of friends?

22 TUESDAY
Moon Age Day 28   Moon Sign Leo

am ....

pm ....
Another strong focus on detail enables you to get all manner of things sorted out today. You are able to look specifically into the very heart of matters and this gives you extra power to alter and influence as necessary. There may now be less of a reliance on the opinions of others, no matter how well intentioned they are.

23 WEDNESDAY
Moon Age Day 0   Moon Sign Leo

am ....

pm ....
It is important to see situations from the position of others, and recent trends make this less likely for the moment. It is true that you have a great ability to get things right on your own, but you don't want those you care about to feel left out in the cold. At least give the impression that you are taking their opinions on board.

24 THURSDAY
Moon Age Day 1   Moon Sign Virgo

am ....

pm ....
A desire to escape responsibility could be the temporary response to the lunar low. As a direct contrast to recent days, you may now be more willing than ever to let those around you take the lead. This is a form of seesawing that they might find difficult to understand. Your kind nature usually wins out in the end though.

25 FRIDAY
Moon Age Day 2   Moon Sign Virgo

am . . . .

pm . . . .
Your capabilities may not be up to the mark today, or at least that is the way you could feel. Don't take on more than is reasonable and give yourself the time you need to rest. There may well be people in your immediate vicinity who have some important and possibly even slightly shocking revelations to impart.

26 SATURDAY
Moon Age Day 3   Moon Sign Libra

am . . . .

pm . . . .
The Sun has now moved into your solar seventh house. This is a more favourable influence with regard to personal relationships. Even if there is some good advice to be had, you need to listen carefully because something that is being said might be deliberately intended to deceive.

27 SUNDAY
Moon Age Day 4   Moon Sign Libra

am . . . .

pm . . . .
Pressure from relationships is now possible, and you would be wise not to react too strongly if it appears that someone is trying to goad you. Getting your own way shouldn't be difficult if you employ a little psychology. There are some unusual trends around at the moment and that means a rather 'different' sort of day.

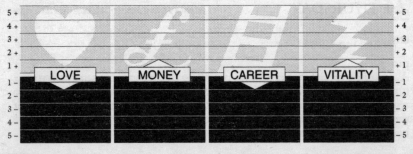

28 MONDAY   *Moon Age Day 5   Moon Sign Libra*

am . . . .

pm . . . .
Relationship matters may not feel too secure under present astrological trends but once again you should discover that if you use a careful approach you can still get what you want from most individuals. It is when others screw up that you have scope to come good, and there are gains to be made as a result of your unique efforts.

29 TUESDAY   *Moon Age Day 6   Moon Sign Scorpio*

am . . . .

pm . . . .
You can make the most of social prospects that are far more rewarding than might have been the case over the last few days. Don't be too keen to take on new challenges, at least until tomorrow. Someone you see very rarely could be making an appearance in your life, and they offer bright and enticing incentives.

30 WEDNESDAY   *Moon Age Day 7   Moon Sign Scorpio*

am . . . .

pm . . . .
Long-distance travel is a possibility for some Pisces subjects at this time, but just about any sort of journey tends to suit you under present trends. Sticking to routines might seem a bore and you need new stimulus in your life if you really want to enjoy the day. Even casual conversations can offer information that is invaluable.

31 THURSDAY   *Moon Age Day 8   Moon Sign Sagittarius*

am . . . .

pm . . . .
There are signs that work and practical matters could occupy your mind a good deal today. There is a strong atmosphere of co-operation about and you can enjoy yourself when with people whose minds work along the same track as yours. Confidence to push yourself forward shouldn't be lacking, either now or approaching the weekend.

1 FRIDAY

Moon Age Day 9   Moon Sign Sagittarius

am . . . .

pm . . . .

A new month starts with encouragement to show a high profile and a determination to get your own way. There are strong incentives where career matters are concerned, but even these pale into insignificance when set against what is on offer socially and romantically. This could be an altogether rewarding day.

2 SATURDAY

Moon Age Day 10   Moon Sign Capricorn

am . . . .

pm . . . .

The greater your social interests today, the more you have scope to enjoy everything that is on offer. Joint ventures are well starred, whether these are associated with work or leisure. Confidence to say and do the right thing is still present, and trends assist you to meet a stream of interesting and stimulating people.

3 SUNDAY

Moon Age Day 11   Moon Sign Capricorn

am . . . .

pm . . . .

A continued high regarding social interest is forecast for today. You probably won't want to get bogged down with tasks you hate and would be wise to leave certain matters until another day. You are probably coming quite close to the end of a specific phase in your life, but this is no time to be rushing your fences.

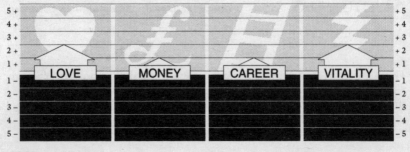

September 2006

YOUR MONTH AT A GLANCE

⊕ = Opportunities are around   ● = Be on the defensive   ◯ = Life is pretty ordinary

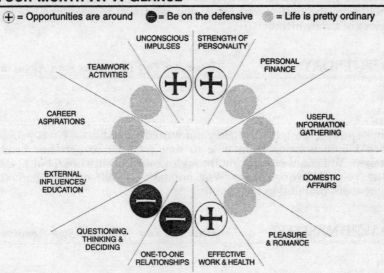

UNCONSCIOUS IMPULSES

STRENGTH OF PERSONALITY

TEAMWORK ACTIVITIES

PERSONAL FINANCE

CAREER ASPIRATIONS

USEFUL INFORMATION GATHERING

EXTERNAL INFLUENCES/ EDUCATION

DOMESTIC AFFAIRS

QUESTIONING, THINKING & DECIDING

ONE-TO-ONE RELATIONSHIPS

EFFECTIVE WORK & HEALTH

PLEASURE & ROMANCE

SEPTEMBER HIGHS AND LOWS

Here I show you how the rhythms of the Moon will affect you this month. Like the tide, your energies and abilities will rise and fall with its pattern. When it is above the centre line, go for it, when it is below, you should be resting.

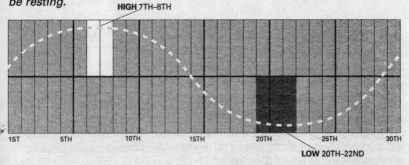

HIGH 7TH–8TH

1ST   5TH   10TH   15TH   20TH   25TH   30TH

LOW 20TH–22ND

119

4 MONDAY
Moon Age Day 12   Moon Sign Capricorn

am ....

pm ....
Some of your most successful hours of the month can be achieved today as you work alongside others. There is the possibility for a sort of 'oneness' that might have been missing in working relationships recently. Away from the professional scene, you can afford to accommodate the wishes of family members.

5 TUESDAY
Moon Age Day 13   Moon Sign Aquarius

am ....

pm ....
Time spent in solitude is certainly not wasted around now. Pisces people need a little isolation from time to time in order to get their heads straight. You could be thinking through all sorts of situations, but in the main you need to meditate. Why not take yourself off to a park or somewhere beautiful in the country?

6 WEDNESDAY
Moon Age Day 14   Moon Sign Aquarius

am ....

pm ....
Try to avoid useless conflicts in relationships or at work. You are probably still not really in the mood to throw yourself fully into any situation that means aggression or confusion. There are ways around any situation if you look carefully, and today does offer plenty in the way of personal happiness, even if practical situations are difficult.

7 THURSDAY
Moon Age Day 15   Moon Sign Pisces

am ....

pm ....
Things change rapidly this month, and today is no exception. From being potentially isolated and introspective, the lunar high could be like being fired out of a cannon. All your enthusiasm comes together to allow forward progress in a number of different ways. Friends might offer some very important practical assistance.

8 FRIDAY
Moon Age Day 16   Moon Sign Pisces

am . . . .

pm . . . .
This would be an excellent time to take a leading role and to show people
what you are made of. There's nothing quiet about Pisces today, and you
have what it takes to share your unique ideas with anyone who will listen.
You can also afford to push your luck more than has been the case so far
this month.

9 SATURDAY
Moon Age Day 17   Moon Sign Aries

am . . . .

pm . . . .
Work-wise and financially, your power to attract just the right
circumstances remains particularly strong. The same positive trends
surround your personal life and it is possible that romance flourishes at
the moment. Conventions might not seem so appealing, and there is
little doubt that you are now doing your own thing.

10 SUNDAY
Moon Age Day 18   Moon Sign Aries

am . . . .

pm . . . .
Trends suggest you might be up against a few challenges when it comes
to keeping yourself organised today. It's late in the year for a springclean,
but that is what elements of your life actually need. Don't burden
yourself with too many obligations because you need the time to
straighten out whatever is bothering you.

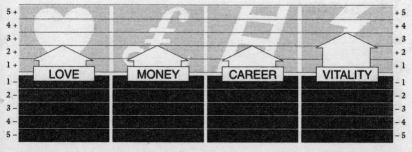

11 MONDAY
Moon Age Day 19   Moon Sign Taurus

am . . . .

pm . . . .

Watch out for new information that comes along that is related to a particular personal plan that might have been on your mind for a while. This is a time during which you can get your ideas across to others in a very effective way. The responses you get from them should prove positive and inspiring.

12 TUESDAY
Moon Age Day 20   Moon Sign Taurus

am . . . .

pm . . . .

You can enjoy an improved social and romantic period whilst the Sun remains in your solar seventh house. The odd, the unusual and the downright weird might have a particular fascination for you under present trends, so don't be surprised if at least a few people look at you askance around this time.

13 WEDNESDAY
Moon Age Day 21   Moon Sign Gemini

am . . . .

pm . . . .

You might be just a little too sensitive to what others think about you now. This temporary trend is brought about by the position of the Moon, which also inclines you to be rather too worried about any form of competition. Just keep telling yourself that you are equal to the task and all should be well.

14 THURSDAY
Moon Age Day 22   Moon Sign Gemini

am . . . .

pm . . . .

There seems to be plenty of potential for good times in all relationships now. Making new friends shouldn't be at all difficult and you can make yourself flavour of the month as far as most people are concerned. Your natural shyness won't be an obstacle under present trends and you practically shine in social situations.

15 FRIDAY
Moon Age Day 23   Moon Sign Cancer

am . . . .

pm . . . .
This is a time for renewal and a period during which you can dump anything that hasn't been working the way you would have wished. If this seems a little cavalier and perhaps even brutal, just think about what will happen if you keep working on projects that don't have a hope of working out the way you would wish.

16 SATURDAY
Moon Age Day 24   Moon Sign Cancer

am . . . .

pm . . . .
Creative self-expression is an important factor in your life around this time. Exciting social and romantic opportunities exist for the weekend, though you will have to make the most of them and shouldn't hold back when it comes to seizing the moment. The fulfilment of a particular wish could be high on your agenda.

17 SUNDAY
Moon Age Day 25   Moon Sign Cancer

am . . . .

pm . . . .
Your feelings may well be stimulated by the chance meetings that come along. Intuition is particularly strong right now and you probably won't want to dwell too much on logic and common sense. There are times when it is important for Pisces to do what simply seems right, and today is such an interlude.

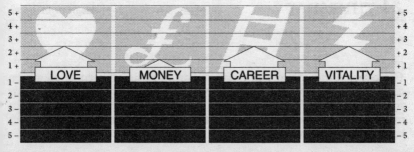

18 MONDAY
Moon Age Day 26   Moon Sign Leo

am . . . .

pm . . . .
You might try to bring a bit more subtlety to certain situations today, though lacking this particular skill is not generally a problem for your birth sign. There is just a possibility that you are not fully taking into account the strength of feeling coming from others. You can blame the position of Mars for this slight hiccup.

19 TUESDAY
Moon Age Day 27   Moon Sign Leo

am . . . .

pm . . . .
Almost everything powerful in your solar chart today is about being efficient. You would be wise to deal with matters one at a time and in the order of their importance. If you try to complete all tasks at the same time you are likely to get yourself in a frightful muddle. You can attract assistance if you decide you need it.

20 WEDNESDAY
Moon Age Day 28   Moon Sign Virgo

am . . . .

pm . . . .
There is likely to be a degree of uncertainty around for the next few days. This comes from the position of the Moon in your opposite zodiac sign. Instead of getting on with anything new, your best response is to deal with situations that are nearly resolved and clear the decks for actions that come towards the end of the week.

21 THURSDAY
Moon Age Day 29   Moon Sign Virgo

am . . . .

pm . . . .
Get as much rest as you can today and avoid being stressed by taking on more than is necessary. You could be a little short-tempered and probably won't have the amount of patience that usually typifies your nature. Your imagination remains strong, a fact that can prove to be of tremendous use in all sorts of ways.

22 FRIDAY
Moon Age Day 0   Moon Sign Virgo

am . . . .

pm . . . .
Even if you are still not on top form, you can improve things as the day goes on. Take situations one at a time and don't be worried about having to seek a little assistance, especially in a professional sense. You can be very diplomatic and can make others feel that by helping you they are doing something worthwhile.

23 SATURDAY
Moon Age Day 1   Moon Sign Libra

am . . . .

pm . . . .
A joint financial issue can be addressed today. You have what it takes to be much more positive than has been the case since the beginning of the week and can even afford to take the odd chance. This should not be a weekend that is simply about getting on, but rather a time during which you can find some personal enjoyment.

24 SUNDAY
Moon Age Day 2   Moon Sign Libra

am . . . .

pm . . . .
Do exercise some caution when you are dealing with people you know to be a little touchy. It isn't anything you are doing that throws a spanner in the works, but there are probably difficulties associated with close attachments. It might be better to spend more time with friends today and less with relatives.

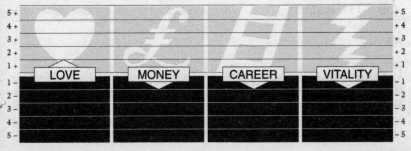

25 MONDAY
Moon Age Day 3   Moon Sign Scorpio

am . . . .

pm . . . .
You can make sure your social life is on a roll at the beginning of this week, and the only real difficulty is likely to be in trying to get everything done that represents practical necessities. One or two jobs might have to be shelved because you are far keener to enjoy your interactions with others than you are to be working.

26 TUESDAY
Moon Age Day 4   Moon Sign Scorpio

am . . . .

pm . . . .
The time has come to put a great deal of effort into establishing your own security. Wherever any setbacks arise you need to remain positive because it is possible you are not showing enough confidence in yourself under present trends. Friends can be especially warm and loving – and in some cases stifling!

27 WEDNESDAY
Moon Age Day 5   Moon Sign Sagittarius

am . . . .

pm . . . .
Trends suggest that today you seek freedom of movement and probably won't take kindly to any situation that finds you being restrained or kept in the same place for too long. It's a sort of mental claustrophobia that sometimes overtakes the Piscean mind. Do anything you have to in order to feel you have sufficient mental space.

28 THURSDAY
Moon Age Day 6   Moon Sign Sagittarius

am . . . .

pm . . . .
You may well have good, practical ideas for professional advancement, but putting them into action could prove just a little problematic now. You need to be very discriminating and even a little ruthless if you really want to get on well. You can afford to tell yourself that you deserve to be listened to because in the main it's true.

29 FRIDAY
Moon Age Day 7   Moon Sign Sagittarius

am . . . .

pm . . . .
Now you can overcome any problems that have been lurking in the corners of your life for the last few weeks. Your ability to see ahead clearly has rarely been better and you will be able to use both practical common sense and your strong intuitive qualities in order to end the working week on a high note.

30 SATURDAY
Moon Age Day 8   Moon Sign Capricorn

am . . . .

pm . . . .
There are good social trends for the weekend. An excellent opportunity exists to form new friendships and to strengthen personal and romantic ties. What you probably won't want to do much today is finish off jobs in and around your home, especially ones that are without personal interest for you.

1 SUNDAY
Moon Age Day 9   Moon Sign Capricorn

am . . . .

pm . . . .
This is another good time to plan and organise joint projects and to find new ways to have fun. Any sort of sporting activity looks especially rewarding under present trends and you could be much more competitive than would usually be the case. You would be wise to stay away from family arguments that you didn't have any part in creating.

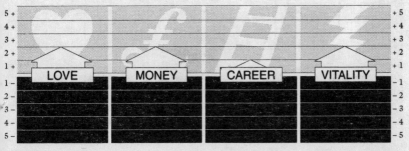

October 2006

YOUR MONTH AT A GLANCE

(+) = Opportunities are around   (—) = Be on the defensive   ⬤ = Life is pretty ordinary

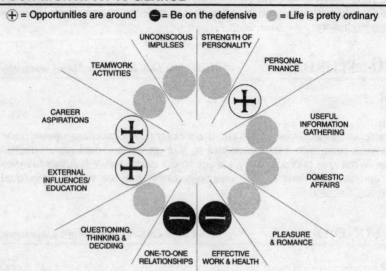

UNCONSCIOUS IMPULSES

STRENGTH OF PERSONALITY

TEAMWORK ACTIVITIES

PERSONAL FINANCE

CAREER ASPIRATIONS

USEFUL INFORMATION GATHERING

EXTERNAL INFLUENCES/ EDUCATION

DOMESTIC AFFAIRS

QUESTIONING, THINKING & DECIDING

PLEASURE & ROMANCE

ONE-TO-ONE RELATIONSHIPS

EFFECTIVE WORK & HEALTH

OCTOBER HIGHS AND LOWS

Here I show you how the rhythms of the Moon will affect you this month. Like the tide, your energies and abilities will rise and fall with its pattern. When it is above the centre line, go for it, when it is below, you should be resting.

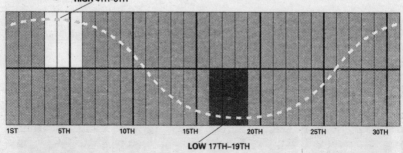

HIGH 4TH–6TH

1ST   5TH   10TH   15TH   20TH   25TH   30TH

LOW 17TH–19TH

2 MONDAY   *Moon Age Day 10   Moon Sign Aquarius*

am . . . .

pm . . . .
Everyday progress may be upset if emotional issues come along to shake
your equilibrium. How you react to these is entirely up to you but there
isn't much point in allowing them to rule your day. If you must worry
about anything, your best approach is to set yourself a time limit for
agitation and then get on with other things.

3 TUESDAY   *Moon Age Day 11   Moon Sign Aquarius*

am . . . .

pm . . . .
You tend to be rather too idealistic for your own good around this time,
which isn't untypical for the zodiac sign of Pisces. A good dose of realism
is called for, together with the recognition that you can actually get life
to go your way if you remain sensible. Why not ask for the advice of
someone older or wiser?

4 WEDNESDAY   *Moon Age Day 12   Moon Sign Pisces*

am . . . .

pm . . . .
The lunar high offers a potentially lucky time and a period during which
things could even fall into place of their own accord. You can gain
support from those who are higher up the ladder than you are and can
use it to make the most of a get-up-and-go interlude that offers new
incentives throughout the day.

5 THURSDAY   *Moon Age Day 13   Moon Sign Pisces*

am . . . .

pm . . . .
The green light is showing and there is no reason at all why you
shouldn't be getting on very well in most spheres of your life. There is a
natural tendency to take up the baton and run with it. If those around
you recognise this fact, they should be more than happy to follow your
lead in most matters.

6 FRIDAY
Moon Age Day 14   Moon Sign Pisces

am ....

pm ....
You have what it takes to ensure that relationship encounters are light-hearted and to alter the rather entrenched ideas of others. Pisces is at its brightest and best just now and there are new incentives to follow. Not everyone you meet will seem to be on your side but you also have strong persuasive powers under present astrological trends.

7 SATURDAY
Moon Age Day 15   Moon Sign Aries

am ....

pm ....
You should now be able to build upon recent successes and the weekend, though sometimes making great demands on you, is one that you will find to be useful and in some way different. Beware of getting bogged down by details, especially in social matters. You can easily get to where you want to go, though you have to flexible.

8 SUNDAY
Moon Age Day 16   Moon Sign Aries

am ....

pm ....
It could be a case of one step forward and two back in some situations today. It might be best to avoid a clash of wills and to stick to your own convictions fairly quietly for the moment. Arrangements may have to be altered and you might get rather annoyed if others don't come up with the goods they have promised.

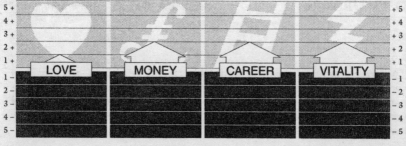

9 MONDAY
Moon Age Day 17   Moon Sign Taurus

am . . . .

pm . . . .
Mental energies are highlighted today and you can get yourself in the right frame of mind to tackle any issues that might have intimidated you in the past. Nothing is missed as you push forward on all fronts and show the world that you are capable of being a go-getter. You might need to be a little circumspect in romantic matters.

10 TUESDAY
Moon Age Day 18   Moon Sign Taurus

am . . . .

pm . . . .
Although you enter a potentially quieter period today, you still have what it takes to be discriminating and shouldn't easily be fooled by anyone. With the Moon now in your solar fourth house you may well decide to find more time for home-based matters and talking more to family members who need your advice.

11 WEDNESDAY
Moon Age Day 19   Moon Sign Gemini

am . . . .

pm . . . .
This would be an excellent day for bringing almost any sort of matter to a head, but you need to be slightly careful how you go about doing it. Trends suggest you may lack some of your usual tact and might not be half as understanding as people expect you to be. Try to show a little sympathy to anyone who fouls up.

12 THURSDAY
Moon Age Day 20   Moon Sign Gemini

am . . . .

pm . . . .
You need to take stock of what is turning out harmoniously for you and perhaps concentrate on those matters. It might seem as though you are a long way from achieving a particular objective, but if you take advantage of a helping hand, this can make all the difference. Slow and steady wins races now.

13 FRIDAY
Moon Age Day 21   Moon Sign Cancer

am ....

pm ....
Relationships issues could be subject to intense emotional moments.
Your best approach is to keep a sense of proportion and try to be steady
in your reactions. What you don't need at the moment is other people
telling you how you should react under any given circumstance. Even
here, you need to be careful not to fire off at them.

14 SATURDAY
Moon Age Day 22   Moon Sign Cancer

am ....

pm ....
A period of higher spirits is on offer, enhancing your sense of adventure.
Little Mercury allows you to bring a dose of excitement into your life for
the weekend and so you may be a lot chattier than has been the case so
far this week. A day to ring the changes where possible and to stay away
from things that bore you intensely.

15 SUNDAY
Moon Age Day 23   Moon Sign Leo

am ....

pm ....
Pressures that exist around you generally leave you unfazed. You have
what it takes to rise above situations that normally pressure you and you
tend to smile a great deal today. When Pisces is optimistic, almost
anything becomes possible and you shouldn't have any trouble attracting
a good deal of positive attention.

16 MONDAY
Moon Age Day 24   Moon Sign Leo

am . . . .

pm . . . .
This is as good a time as any to really enjoy intimate relationships. The position of the planet Venus is ideal for telling the one you love the most just how important they are to you and the reaction you can attract could be very positive. Some Pisceans will be choosing this time to take a well-earned break or even a holiday.

17 TUESDAY
Moon Age Day 25   Moon Sign Virgo

am . . . .

pm . . . .
Daily issues might now look less positive as the lunar low bears down on you. All the same, you have plenty of supporting planets around and that could mean that apart from a slight tendency to look on the black side, you needn't let the lunar low affect your life during October. Don't slow down where major efforts are concerned.

18 WEDNESDAY
Moon Age Day 26   Moon Sign Virgo

am . . . .

pm . . . .
They say a change is as good as a rest and that certainly seems to be the case as far as you are concerned. There is no sense in trying to keep track of everything that is going on around you and it would be advantageous to allow others to take some of the strain in matters that are not of supreme importance.

19 THURSDAY
Moon Age Day 27   Moon Sign Virgo

am . . . .

pm . . . .
Even if you are still feeling somewhat lacking in enterprise and initiative, this temporary trend weakens as today grows older. Now is the time to look at a particular work-related issue in greater detail and if you can use today to do some sort of research, so much the better. A more confident phase is just around the corner.

20 FRIDAY
Moon Age Day 28   Moon Sign Libra

am . . . .

pm . . . .
Personal ambitions may be slightly less focused than you might wish, but that needn't matter if you can take a broad overview of life. You would be wise to concentrate on what you know you can do well at work, but by the time the evening comes along, you should have scope to try something new.

21 SATURDAY
Moon Age Day 0   Moon Sign Libra

am . . . .

pm . . . .
Beware of taking on any more duties than you have to. You are going to work at your best when you know what is expected of you and whilst moving on at your own pace. Any form of supervision probably won't be appreciated because you prefer to do things in your own way. Nevertheless you can remain generally tactful.

22 SUNDAY
Moon Age Day 1   Moon Sign Scorpio

am . . . .

pm . . . .
Once again a bout of sheer optimism is available to you. This is a bit of a roller coaster of a month when it comes to your attitude to life and that might make it somewhat difficult for others to follow your attitude. You might even shock one or two people today with your determination to be cheerful.

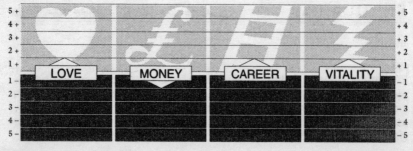

23 MONDAY
Moon Age Day 2   Moon Sign Scorpio

am . . . .

pm . . . .
The Sun has now moved into your solar ninth house, where it remains for the next month or so. This brings a good time for expanding social interests and a period during which you are encouraged to meet as many new faces as you can. For the moment you have scope to make a personal attachment more secure.

24 TUESDAY
Moon Age Day 3   Moon Sign Scorpio

am . . . .

pm . . . .
The time is right to make up your mind about proposed career changes, and if you cannot do so, to look to the advice of people who know the situation and also know you. In the end you have to choose for yourself but the different perspective that can be brought to bear by friends could still be very useful.

25 WEDNESDAY
Moon Age Day 4   Moon Sign Sagittarius

am . . . .

pm . . . .
Though you need to push your own ideas forward under present trends, you should still be prepared to listen to what others think. This is probably one of the very few days of the year on which you could be accused of being selfish, but the accusation is only slightly true. You do have the right to self-choice.

26 THURSDAY
Moon Age Day 5   Moon Sign Sagittarius

am . . . .

pm . . . .
You should now be entering a more mentally fulfilling interlude and the sense of 'movement' in your life is likely to be very welcome. You needn't hold fast to what you know, but can show yourself willing to change when necessary. A definite breeze of opportunity seems to be blowing through your life.

27 FRIDAY
Moon Age Day 6   Moon Sign Capricorn

am . . . .

pm . . . .
There may be a slight sense of restlessness, which is brought about by the very same planetary trends that show promise of new times ahead. If you find yourself jumping about from foot to foot, why not look to do something new and even revolutionary? You might shock some people, but that's no bad thing either.

28 SATURDAY
☿ *Moon Age Day 7   Moon Sign Capricorn*

am . . . .

pm . . . .
Trends suggest that a friend might have some inspiring news. Even if this doesn't have a bearing on your life you should be pleased for them. There are excellent trends around that say 'have a chat with someone you like'. You don't actually have to achieve anything at all today, because life seems to be arranging itself pretty effectively.

29 SUNDAY
☿ *Moon Age Day 8   Moon Sign Aquarius*

am . . . .

pm . . . .
Much is positively highlighted in the world of communication. Meetings offer scope for significant rewards and you need to continue to do all you can to broaden your horizons generally. Routines are definitely for the birds and you can bring a fresh and inspiring quality to almost everything you do.

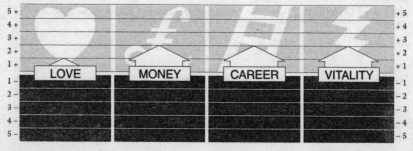

30 MONDAY   ☿   *Moon Age Day 9   Moon Sign Aquarius*

am ....

pm ....
At the start of a new week you have what it takes to remain generally optimistic and to look forward to tasks that normally cause you to be nervous. Pisces is really firing on all cylinders, even if you can't be quite as voluble as you will be by Wednesday. A twelfth-house Moon could hold you back just slightly.

31 TUESDAY   ☿   *Moon Age Day 10   Moon Sign Aquarius*

am ....

pm ....
When it comes to discussions and debate a more relaxed atmosphere is now possible. There may have been times during October when you were tense and didn't communicate quite as well as you might. Those times are now over and you can commit yourself fully to co-operation and to seeing the other person's point of view.

1 WEDNESDAY   ☿   *Moon Age Day 11   Moon Sign Pisces*

am ....

pm ....
A new month coincides with the lunar high and assist you to start November in a very positive frame of mind. A very influential figure may well enter your life at this time and you can show yourself to be generally good at changing with circumstances. You can afford to push your luck much more under prevailing trends.

2 THURSDAY   ☿   *Moon Age Day 12   Moon Sign Pisces*

am ....

pm ....
There is every reason to believe that you can get life to go your way at the moment. Most circumstances seem to be working to your distinct advantage but a lot of this is down to your own positive attitude. Creative potential is especially good and you have what it takes to turn heads in a personal sense.

3 FRIDAY ☿ *Moon Age Day 13   Moon Sign Aries*

am ....

pm ....
Positive trends are still in operation as far as work is concerned and those amongst you who have recently started a new job can use these to get into the groove. With everything to play for in romance too, this should be one of the most positive phases you have encountered for some time.

4 SATURDAY ☿ *Moon Age Day 14   Moon Sign Aries*

am ....

pm ....
Exchanges of ideas that come along today could prove to be quite inspiring. You should make the most of any excitement that is on offer around now, probably brought about by chance meetings or new associations. Sporting Pisces types should really be going for gold under present planetary trends.

5 SUNDAY ☿ *Moon Age Day 15   Moon Sign Taurus*

am ....

pm ....
Trends encourage a strong urge for freedom and the pursuit of unusual adventures. Travel is positively in the spotlight and you may not be content to stay in the same place all the time. With an exciting time possible, you might have trouble keeping up with home-based chores and may decide to rely on the good offices of others.

	LOVE	MONEY	CAREER	VITALITY

November 2006

YOUR MONTH AT A GLANCE

⊕ = Opportunities are around   ⊖ = Be on the defensive   ⬤ = Life is pretty ordinary

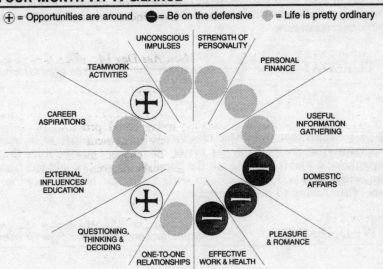

- UNCONSCIOUS IMPULSES
- STRENGTH OF PERSONALITY
- PERSONAL FINANCE
- USEFUL INFORMATION GATHERING
- DOMESTIC AFFAIRS
- PLEASURE & ROMANCE
- EFFECTIVE WORK & HEALTH
- ONE-TO-ONE RELATIONSHIPS
- QUESTIONING, THINKING & DECIDING
- EXTERNAL INFLUENCES/ EDUCATION
- CAREER ASPIRATIONS
- TEAMWORK ACTIVITIES

NOVEMBER HIGHS AND LOWS

Here I show you how the rhythms of the Moon will affect you this month. Like the tide, your energies and abilities will rise and fall with its pattern. When it is above the centre line, go for it, when it is below, you should be resting. **HIGH** 1ST–2ND   **HIGH** 28TH–29TH

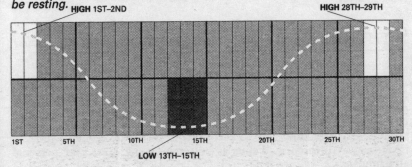

1ST   5TH   10TH   15TH   20TH   25TH   30TH

LOW 13TH–15TH

6 MONDAY ☿ *Moon Age Day 16   Moon Sign Taurus*

am . . . .

pm . . . .
This is a period during which it ought to be possible for you to attend to many different things at the same time. You have what it takes to show the best of your nature to the world at large, and very little should faze you. You can also ensure that significant attention is being paid to your opinions around now.

7 TUESDAY ☿ *Moon Age Day 17   Moon Sign Gemini*

am . . . .

pm . . . .
There are signs that the advice of a loved one could prove to be very important. You are probably far better off listening today rather than being the one who is handing out the homilies. Routines could feel fairly comfortable and you may decide to settle for second-best on occasions, rather than having to push yourself.

8 WEDNESDAY ☿ *Moon Age Day 18   Moon Sign Gemini*

am . . . .

pm . . . .
Venus offers a potentially rewarding period during which you are fully in contact with the world beyond your door. You can tap into more energy than was available yesterday, and part of this comes about because other people seem to trust your judgement so much. This would be a good day for a journey.

9 THURSDAY ☿ *Moon Age Day 19   Moon Sign Cancer*

am . . . .

pm . . . .
A discussion could be the cause of some irritation, which is why it might be best not to get too involved today if you can avoid doing so. A day to stick to what you know and to keep to your own little corner if you feel in any way threatened. Venus is still supporting you, and personal attachments are well starred.

10 FRIDAY ☿ *Moon Age Day 20 Moon Sign Cancer*

am . . . .

pm . . . .
A varied and interesting life now beckons again and some of the slightly
negative trends of the last few days seem to be disappearing. You have the
ability to function extremely well in company and can find exactly the
right words to influence those around you, particularly at work. The
evening offers you scope to enjoy a total change.

11 SATURDAY ☿ *Moon Age Day 21 Moon Sign Leo*

am . . . .

pm . . . .
There are some excellent influences around when it comes to looking and
planning ahead. With plenty of positive feedback available and a desire to
break the bounds of the credible, you can make this a rewarding and
stimulating interlude. The opinions of friends could vary wildly now.

12 SUNDAY ☿ *Moon Age Day 22 Moon Sign Leo*

am . . . .

pm . . . .
Discussions to do with travel can be the cause of irritation, especially if
others are not on the same wavelength as you are. You need to be rather
more assertive than of late if you don't want to be left at the back of any
particular queue. The closer you get to finishing a specific task, the more
awkward it might seem to be.

13 MONDAY ☿ *Moon Age Day 23   Moon Sign Virgo*

am . . . .

pm . . . .
It is towards your social life that trends encourage you to turn your mind, and travel arrangements could be your second-best area just at the moment. There's no harm in standing still for a while. All Pisces people need interludes during which they can meditate and plan for the future. The lunar low offers just such a time.

14 TUESDAY ☿ *Moon Age Day 24   Moon Sign Virgo*

am . . . .

pm . . . .
Plans of action are not favoured as the lunar low continues. You may not be on top form and could seem to be walking through treacle, especially where your professional life is concerned. This is nothing but a short interlude, and so there is no need to react adversely to present happenings.

15 WEDNESDAY ☿ *Moon Age Day 25   Moon Sign Virgo*

am . . . .

pm . . . .
Certain issues at the moment are like fruit – you can't force them on but have to wait until they are ripe. Trying to rush will only lead to mistakes, whereas if you are patient, you can make sure that what you want will come your way. You would be wise to keep an open mind about travel plans for the future, but don't commit yourself yet.

16 THURSDAY ☿ *Moon Age Day 26   Moon Sign Libra*

am . . . .

pm . . . .
It is possible that emotional relationships and issues between yourself and your partner can seem more trouble than they are worth at first today. You need to keep life simple and you haven't really got the time or the inclination to be involved in disputes at work either. A day to stick to your corner, at least until later.

17 FRIDAY   ☿   *Moon Age Day 27   Moon Sign Libra*

am . . . .

pm . . . .
Venus is now in your solar tenth house and that could prove to be of
significant help at work. Things may not have been going exactly the way
you would have wished of late and incentives have been lacking. Now,
with a combination of input from others together with your own new
ideas, you can get things back on track.

18 SATURDAY   ☿   *Moon Age Day 28   Moon Sign Scorpio*

am . . . .

pm . . . .
You can make this a time of versatility and mental dexterity. Having
several interests on the go at the same time could be rewarding, and there
isn't any doubt about your ability to turn heads in social and romantic
situations. Just be careful you don't inspire a little unnecessary jealousy
in someone else.

19 SUNDAY   *Moon Age Day 29   Moon Sign Scorpio*

am . . . .

pm . . . .
This is a time during which you need to think expansively and to work to
the best of your abilities. Although this might not be particularly relevant
in a working sense today, you do have the ability to get things sorted out
for the week ahead, because the positive trends surrounding you now will
be around for a few days.

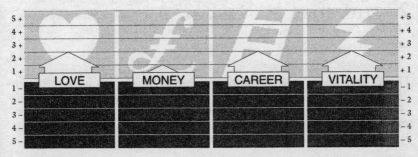

20 MONDAY
Moon Age Day 0   Moon Sign Scorpio

am . . . .

pm . . . .
It might be quite easy for others to take exception to your views today but that is hardly your fault. You can't please all of the people all of the time, and there's no real point in trying to do so. If you stick to your guns and remain confident, you can persuade those who are important to follow your reasoning.

21 TUESDAY
Moon Age Day 1   Moon Sign Sagittarius

am . . . .

pm . . . .
You would do well to follow innovative ideas that have potential to be quite profitable in the fullness of time. The best guide at the moment is your own intuition, which is especially strong. The area of life most worthy of concentration is work, but that doesn't mean you can't have a good time later.

22 WEDNESDAY
Moon Age Day 2   Moon Sign Sagittarius

am . . . .

pm . . . .
Planetary influences now suggest that certain meaningful ambitions are within your reach. You have what it takes to get higher-ups to offer a helping hand perhaps even new incentives and responsibilities. It is up to you to prove that you are equal to the task. This could also be a good time romantically.

23 THURSDAY
Moon Age Day 3   Moon Sign Capricorn

am . . . .

pm . . . .
This is likely to be one of those days during which you have scope to shine like the morning star. Just about everything possible comes together in an astrological sense to offer some of the best incentives of the month. In particular you can make sure that you are being looked at by others with a combination of admiration and awe.

24 FRIDAY
Moon Age Day 4   Moon Sign Capricorn

am . . . .

pm . . . .
Group, teamwork and all social matters can be made to work well for you
now. If you are determined to keep life varied and interesting, you can
get plenty of help to do so. Chances are that you will do equally well at
work or in social situations. You might have to be just a little careful not
to give someone the wrong romantic impression.

25 SATURDAY
Moon Age Day 5   Moon Sign Aquarius

am . . . .

pm . . . .
Remember that you can't please everyone and you shouldn't go far
wrong today. There is just a chance that someone thinks you are too
confident for your own good, perhaps with regard to a single issue. Try
to explain yourself, but not for too long. At the end of the day you need
your energy to prove your opinions.

26 SUNDAY
Moon Age Day 6   Moon Sign Aquarius

am . . . .

pm . . . .
If efficiency is not as pronounced as you would wish today, thank the
position of the Moon in your solar twelfth house. This would not be the
best time to try and move people who are determined to be stubborn.
Save your resources for situations that are already starting to go the way
you would wish.

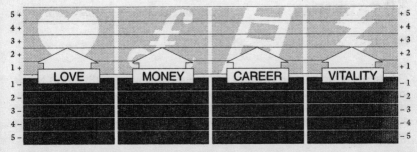

27 MONDAY

Moon Age Day 7   Moon Sign Aquarius

am . . . .

pm . . . .

You may be on to a winner where career matters are concerned. For some days now the Sun has been in your solar tenth house and from this position it brings new incentives and an ability to cut through any red tape that has got in your way recently. An open attitude is best in most situations under present influences.

28 TUESDAY

Moon Age Day 8   Moon Sign Pisces

am . . . .

pm . . . .

The lunar high arrives and should bring with it the chance to make this one of the more fortunate periods during November. You can be especially intuitive now and very resourceful. This is a time during which you really do have to believe in yourself, because when it is obvious that you do, you can convince everyone else to fall in line.

29 WEDNESDAY

Moon Age Day 9   Moon Sign Pisces

am . . . .

pm . . . .

A day to take advantage of the very promising influences that stand around you now. You can be bright, easy-going, adventurous and very good to know. What more could the world ask? Most important of all you need to believe in yourself because there is very little that lies beyond your capabilities now.

30 THURSDAY

Moon Age Day 10   Moon Sign Aries

am . . . .

pm . . . .

The opportunities for monetary advancement are especially good at the moment. You can afford to chance your arm a little more and once again you need to rely on your intuition to offer the best incentives. When it comes to your personal life it looks as though you can turn this into a varied but quite stimulating time.

1 FRIDAY
Moon Age Day 11   Moon Sign Aries

am . . . .

pm . . . .
Trends encourage you to be assertive and even quite outspoken around
now. The present position of Mars in your solar chart calls upon you to
let people know the way you feel about almost everything and this can
prove shocking to them if it's not what they expect from you. Still, it
doesn't do any harm to shake things up now and again!

2 SATURDAY
Moon Age Day 12   Moon Sign Taurus

am . . . .

pm . . . .
If you would prefer to be on the move this weekend, you may decide to
involve yourself in a variety of different interests. All the same, there
might be one special goal that is worth pursuing and you need to keep
this close to the forefront of your mind. Chance meetings could have far-
reaching implications.

3 SUNDAY
Moon Age Day 13   Moon Sign Taurus

am . . . .

pm . . . .
This could prove to be a rather fortunate day in a professional sense,
though this won't be of any use unless you work during the weekend. On
a social level you have scope to mix with new friends, or maybe to take a
new look at old contacts. There might not be any financial rewards today
but the personal ones look good.

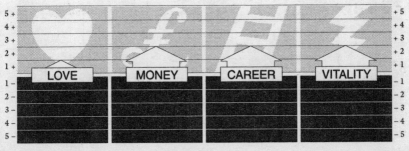

December 2006

YOUR MONTH AT A GLANCE

⊕ = Opportunities are around   ⊖ = Be on the defensive   ⬤ = Life is pretty ordinary

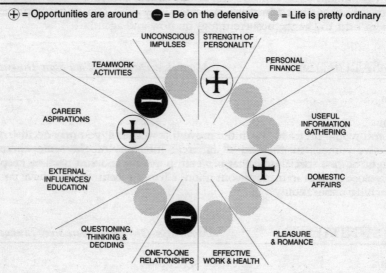

DECEMBER HIGHS AND LOWS

Here I show you how the rhythms of the Moon will affect you this month. Like the tide, your energies and abilities will rise and fall with its pattern. When it is above the centre line, go for it, when it is below, you should be resting.

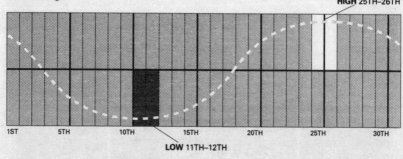

HIGH 25TH–26TH

LOW 11TH–12TH

4 MONDAY
Moon Age Day 14   Moon Sign Gemini

am . . . .

pm . . . .
Though there might be a few let-downs to contend with today, in the main you can make the day run fairly smoothly. You can probably rely pretty much on the good offices of friends and might also discover something to your advantage at work. It's really a case of keeping your eyes open to get the best from today.

5 TUESDAY
Moon Age Day 15   Moon Sign Gemini

am . . . .

pm . . . .
You are entering a forward-looking and progressive little phase that lasts between now and the end of the week. At the moment you are most responsive to the position of the Sun in your solar chart and there are good potentials to reap rewards of one sort or another. A day to keep up a sensible pace with any subject matter that puzzles you.

6 WEDNESDAY
Moon Age Day 16   Moon Sign Cancer

am . . . .

pm . . . .
It is now possible for you to elicit the very best of responses from loved ones. Domestic matters could be on your mind but that needn't prevent you from making generally good progress in practical matters too. Keep an eye open for the chance to pursue a little adventure.

7 THURSDAY
Moon Age Day 17   Moon Sign Cancer

am . . . .

pm . . . .
Where professional details are concerned you should be very much on the ball. You needn't wait to be asked today but can afford to take what you need from life as your right. This up-front behaviour on your part might be a bit of a puzzle to some of those you mix with, but it never does any harm to upset the applecart just a little.

8 FRIDAY

Moon Age Day 18   Moon Sign Cancer

am ....

pm ....
This ought to be a very favourable day for all practical matters, but beware of leaving current projects until it's too late. You need to be flexible at the moment and to respond to situations as and when necessary. Romance could be available later and you can plan now for a generally good weekend ahead.

9 SATURDAY

Moon Age Day 19   Moon Sign Leo

am ....

pm ....
Trends assist you to benefit greatly today from discussions, and you need to stay generally well informed about the world. If not everyone is giving you the credit due for your successes in the recent past, that might be because they are slightly envious. Your oldest and best friends should come up trumps every time.

10 SUNDAY

Moon Age Day 20   Moon Sign Leo

am ....

pm ....
Now is the time to look for someone who is more than willing to put themselves out on your behalf, just when their opinions are worth a lot. Attitude is all-important if you are facing issues over which you have little experience, together with a willingness to be flexible.

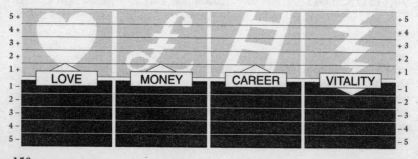

11 MONDAY
Moon Age Day 21   Moon Sign Virgo

am ....

pm ....
Don't expect too many miracles today. With the lunar low around it might be just about all you can manage to maintain the forward motion in your life. If your plans are modest and you keep yourself to yourself, you can best ensure that the Moon does very little to shake your equilibrium.

12 TUESDAY
Moon Age Day 22   Moon Sign Virgo

am ....

pm ....
Your power to influence life in any remarkable way remains limited. It would be best to find your own little corner today and to do what pleases you. If you have any major plans it would be sensible to put these on hold, at least until tomorrow. If Pisces is in a quiet frame of mind, that could be very difficult to alter.

13 WEDNESDAY
Moon Age Day 23   Moon Sign Libra

am ....

pm ....
It would be all too easy today to get caught up in disagreements regarding the various rights and wrongs of situations. You need to ask yourself if, at the end of the day, anything will be changed as a result of these differences of opinion. Better by far to maintain your cheerful attitude and to refuse to be drawn.

14 THURSDAY
Moon Age Day 24   Moon Sign Libra

am ....

pm ....
The Moon is now in your solar eighth house, a planetary position that is said to be good for solving personal problems. Perhaps someone close is more likely to listen to your opinions now, or it could simply be that they recognise your own attitude as being constructive. Younger family members might also need your attention.

15 FRIDAY
Moon Age Day 25   Moon Sign Libra

am . . . .

pm . . . .
It may have slipped your mind somewhat across the last week, but Christmas is just around the corner. In amongst what could be a very busy life, you need to get those festive details sorted out. What probably isn't happening too much this year is the deeply nostalgic frame of mind that often turns up for Pisces at this time.

16 SATURDAY
Moon Age Day 26   Moon Sign Scorpio

am . . . .

pm . . . .
There could well be a sense of restlessness in the air, so perhaps some mental stimulation would help you to feel good about life generally. Don't wait for this to come along, but find it yourself in your everyday life. You have what it takes to convince others to follow your lead, so don't sit around but remain active.

17 SUNDAY
Moon Age Day 27   Moon Sign Scorpio

am . . . .

pm . . . .
Social matters look particularly favourable and you can make this a very happy sort of Sunday, unless of course you have to work. Professional trends are not quite so well starred and it could be that too much is being demanded of you. If you can spend time with family and friends, it is probably with them that you can find the most fun.

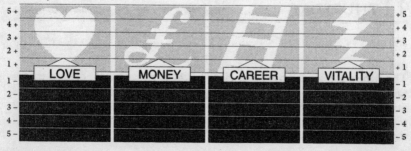

18 MONDAY
Moon Age Day 28   Moon Sign Sagittarius

am . . . .

pm . . . .
Dealings with professional contacts can bring some significant success, but you do need to be patient because situations may not mature too quickly with Christmas in view. Even if you are very definitely in a mood to push on with practical matters, the world around you could seem to be already giving itself up to celebrations.

19 TUESDAY
Moon Age Day 29   Moon Sign Sagittarius

am . . . .

pm . . . .
It is what you know that helps you to get ahead now. You need to rely on your own knowledge, together with a big helping of intuition, in order to make the right moves. It doesn't matter what others tell you because in the end you can afford to approach life in your own way. Be diplomatic by all means, but plough your own furrow.

20 WEDNESDAY
Moon Age Day 0   Moon Sign Sagittarius

am . . . .

pm . . . .
Mars remains in your solar tenth house and from this position it can continue to offer a boost to professional matters in particular. You have scope to get on with things, but there could be hold-ups caused by situations beyond your own control. The result might be a little frustration that needs to be dealt with carefully.

21 THURSDAY
Moon Age Day 1   Moon Sign Capricorn

am . . . .

pm . . . .
A great period business-wise and probably less restricted than yesterday because Mercury has now also moved into your tenth house. You should find it easier to explain yourself, and what is even better is that people are probably listening to you. There are still some restrictions possible, but these relate to the time of year.

22 FRIDAY
Moon Age Day 2   Moon Sign Capricorn

am ....

pm ....
Trends indicate that what is happening in your social life now becomes more important and more rewarding. It could be that you have decided that to make any serious ground professionally, with Christmas so close, is something of a waste of time. If friends have suggestions to make, you might find them hard to refuse.

23 SATURDAY
Moon Age Day 3   Moon Sign Aquarius

am ....

pm ....
The Moon is now in your solar twelfth house and that brings a slight tendency to daydream. This is where the real nostalgia at the heart of the Pisces nature begins to make itself felt. Your mind is inclined to go back to Christmases from the past. That's fine, as long as you don't convince yourself that things were better then.

24 SUNDAY
Moon Age Day 4   Moon Sign Aquarius

am ....

pm ....
Your social life enables you to bring out the best in yourself, but you could still be just a little introspective and not quite as inclined to let your hair down as will be the case by tomorrow. You might decide to settle for a quiet evening, maybe with your partner or the family, but that can bring its own form of joy.

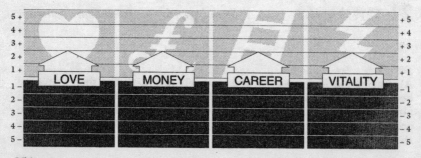

25 MONDAY
Moon Age Day 5   Moon Sign Pisces

am . . . .

pm . . . .
The lunar high coincides with the Christmas period for you this year, and that can help you to make this a very happy time. You should have sufficient energy to keep up with the needs of your family and can be the life and soul of any party that is taking place around you. In most situations you can automatically lead today.

26 TUESDAY
Moon Age Day 6   Moon Sign Pisces

am . . . .

pm . . . .
You have scope to remain on a general high and to attract others with your sparkling personality and natural warmth. There should be few frustrations in your life around this time and you might also be fairly lucky. Don't worry about keeping a sense of proportion. You don't need one today!

27 WEDNESDAY
Moon Age Day 7   Moon Sign Aries

am . . . .

pm . . . .
You can afford to maintain the very friendly approach that others find attractive. It doesn't matter who you mix with at this time because you are very adaptable. Attitude is very important if you are facing new situations, which could easily be the case under present trends. There are signs that family members could be slightly overbearing.

28 THURSDAY
Moon Age Day 8   Moon Sign Aries

am . . . .

pm . . . .
Teamwork activities are your most favoured area under present planetary trends, though if you know how to enjoy yourself, social possibilities are the best for today. Don't worry about arranging things too carefully because it is likely to be the sudden and last-minute gatherings and functions that are the most exciting.

29 FRIDAY
Moon Age Day 9   Moon Sign Taurus

am ....

pm ....
The ordinary daily comings and goings of life may well have a particular appeal, particularly if you are slightly tired of having a good time. You need a sense of normality in your life and have what it takes to tackle all manner of domestic chores with great cheerfulness. Beware of counting too much on people who are unknown to you.

30 SATURDAY
Moon Age Day 10   Moon Sign Taurus

am ....

pm ....
An added lift to friendship is now possible, thanks to the position of Venus in your solar chart. 'The more, the merrier' is likely to be your adage and you can settle down to celebrations much more readily than might have been the case yesterday. Make the most of romance that could come knocking on your door any time now.

31 SUNDAY
Moon Age Day 11   Moon Sign Taurus

am ....

pm ....
Personal and family life seem to be the most rewarding areas for the last day of the year. You could well be taking a journey down memory lane, but there is nothing strange about this for Pisces, particularly at this time of year. Stand by to enjoy yourself in the evening by all means, but keep the festivities within sensible bounds.

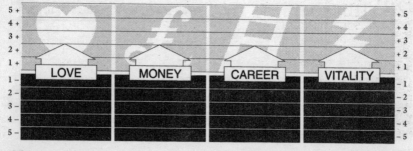

RISING SIGNS FOR PISCES

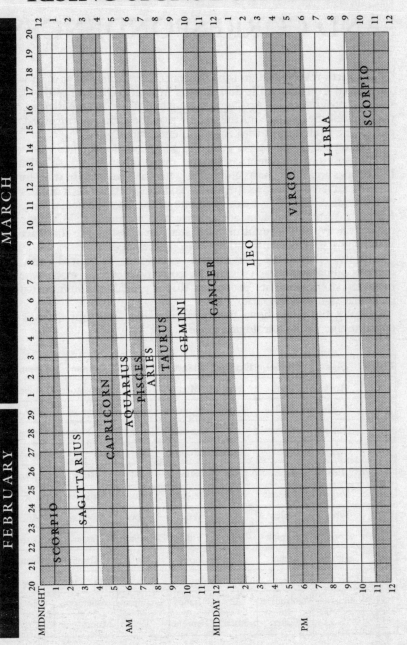

THE ZODIAC, PLANETS AND CORRESPONDENCES

The Earth revolves around the Sun once every calendar year, so when viewed from Earth the Sun appears in a different part of the sky as the year progresses. In astrology, these parts of the sky are divided into the signs of the zodiac and this means that the signs are organised in a circle. The circle begins with Aries and ends with Pisces.

Taking the zodiac sign as a starting point, astrologers then work with all the positions of planets, stars and many other factors to calculate horoscopes and birth charts and tell us what the stars have in store for us.

The table below shows the planets and Elements for each of the signs of the zodiac. Each sign belongs to one of the four Elements: Fire, Air, Earth or Water. Fire signs are creative and enthusiastic; Air signs are mentally active and thoughtful; Earth signs are constructive and practical; Water signs are emotional and have strong feelings.

It also shows the metals and gemstones associated with, or corresponding with, each sign. The correspondence is made when a metal or stone possesses properties that are held in common with a particular sign of the zodiac.

Finally, the table shows the opposite of each star sign – this is the opposite sign in the astrological circle.

Placed	Sign	Symbol	Element	Planet	Metal	Stone	Opposite
1	Aries	Ram	Fire	Mars	Iron	Bloodstone	Libra
2	Taurus	Bull	Earth	Venus	Copper	Sapphire	Scorpio
3	Gemini	Twins	Air	Mercury	Mercury	Tiger's Eye	Sagittarius
4	Cancer	Crab	Water	Moon	Silver	Pearl	Capricorn
5	Leo	Lion	Fire	Sun	Gold	Ruby	Aquarius
6	Virgo	Maiden	Earth	Mercury	Mercury	Sardonyx	Pisces
7	Libra	Scales	Air	Venus	Copper	Sapphire	Aries
8	Scorpio	Scorpion	Water	Pluto	Plutonium	Jasper	Taurus
9	Sagittarius	Archer	Fire	Jupiter	Tin	Topaz	Gemini
10	Capricorn	Goat	Earth	Saturn	Lead	Black Onyx	Cancer
11	Aquarius	Waterbearer	Air	Uranus	Uranium	Amethyst	Leo
12	Pisces	Fishes	Water	Neptune	Tin	Moonstone	Virgo

Your very own personal horoscope by **Old Moore**

The timeless wisdom of **Old Moore** *can now be interpreted by computer – to give you an astounding wealth of insights and revelations.*

A t last, the huge analytical power of the computer has been harnessed to the legendary forecasting skills of **Old Moore**.

By revealing the mysteries held within your own astrological chart, you will gain a unique insight into yourself and find a new path to your future which you yourself can influence.

It is based on the **Old Moore** prediction system, which has proved to be uniquely successful and accurate for over three hundred years.

Now it focuses entirely on *YOU*. The result is your very own *character profile and forecast horoscope* for the next twelve months.

Send off the coupon below with your remittance of £17.00, and enjoy a unique view of your future.

OLD MOORE HOROSCOPE

12-month Horoscope Book – *personal to you* – for only **£17.00** INCLUDING P&P.

* Most detailed astral reading of its kind.

* CHARACTER PROFILE explores the depths of your true self.

* PERSONAL FORECAST predicts ways to improve your happiness and success.

* In a tradition of accurate forecasting since 1697.

YOUR DATE WITH DESTINY...

UNIQUE GIFT IDEA – SEND THIS COUPON NOW!

To BJA, PO Box 1321, SLOUGH PDO, Berkshire SL1 5YD. I enclose £17.00 for my **Old Moore** Personal Horoscope (Overseas £19.00, €30 or $29.95 USA.)

(Make cheques payable to BJA. Please allow 28 days for delivery.)

NAME _____

ADDRESS _____

_____

_____

POST CODE _____

Please print your birth details:

DATE AND YEAR _____

TIME (IF KNOWN) _____

PLACE _____

If you prefer not to receive mailings from companies other than those connected to Old Moore, please tick the box ❑

09068 229 723: *ring Old Moore now* – for the most authentic personal phone horoscope ever made available

Then just tap in your own birth date …

… and benefit from the wisdom of the centuries

The uncanny foresight of Britain's No1 astrologer – focused directly on your own individual *birth-chart*

Unique personalised reading

There's never been a better way to exploit your personal horoscope opportunities.

Old Moore now has a massive new computer with which he can produce a personal forecast based on the actual day of your birth. No other astro phone service can produce this level of accuracy.

Any day of the week, Old Moore can update you on the planetary influences which surround you and point up the opportunities which will be open to you.

Unique record of prediction

The principles of astro interpretation laid down by Old Moore three centuries ago have proved amazingly reliable and accurate right up to the present day. That's how the unique Old Moore system can be harnessed to analyse your own personal world.

Meet Old Moore any day

For just 60p per minute you can hear this authoritative overview of your life, work and happiness. Not the usual 'fortune-telling' patter, but enlightened insights into how best to exploit the day and the *immediate*.

Remember, unlike any other phone astrologer, Old Moore will ask you for the *day, month and year* of your birth, to give you the most individual advice and predictions ever possible.

So touch hands with the immortal Old Moore. Ring this number and get a truly personalised forecast, from the world's most acclaimed astrologer.

This service is only available on a touch tone button phone.

09068 229 723

Calls cost 60p per minute at all times.
(Charges may be higher for payphones and non-BT networks.)